Praise for *Four Gospels, One Jesus:*

"A wonderful book. . . . Clear exposition, creative method, abundant theological and literary insights, and valuable engagement with the history of interpretation. . . . May it stay in print forever!"

— MARGARET M. MITCHELL
McCormick Theological Seminary

"Engaging. . . . *Four Gospels, One Jesus* is to be recommended for its creative and accessible approach to reading the Gospels as narrative christologies."

— *Toronto Journal of Theology*

"A rare merger of the very best of modern biblical scholarship with a readable and engaging telling of the Gospel portraits of Jesus particularly aimed at a popular audience."

— *Anglican Theological Review*

"Masterly. . . . Burridge makes reading the Gospels exciting."

— *On Being*

"Fresh and pleasing in presentation. . . . This is a very useful and well-written little book, excellent for beginning students or lay study groups."

— *Sewanee Theological Review*

"Will be welcomed by any pastor or teacher whose flock has become discouraged in the face of historical criticism."

— *Pro Ecclesia*

"A fine introduction to the distinctive portrait of Jesus provided by each of the Gospels. . . . This book should prove to be a very helpful window into Gospel scholarship for many readers."
— *Reformed Theological Review*

"Though this book is ultimately about the one Jesus, readers will receive the benefit of responsible and readable scholarship concerning the authorship, sources, and criticism of the biblical narrative."
— *The Living Church*

"A scholarly primer on the Gospels. . . . Valuable for undergraduate students or for general readers without a background in New Testament studies."

— *Christian Librarian*

"Lucid and appealing. . . . This is a study of the Gospels that needs to be added to theological libraries for beginners."

— *Vidyajyoti*

"A fresh look at the Gospels as biographies. . . . It is a good resource for serious Bible students and should be especially helpful to pastors and other leaders of Bible studies based on the four Gospels."
— *Lutheran Libraries*

Four Gospels, One Jesus?
A Symbolic Reading

RICHARD A. BURRIDGE

William B. Eerdmans Publishing Company
Grand Rapids, Michigan

This edition published 1994
through special arrangement with SPCK
Wm. B. Eerdmans Publishing Co.
255 Jefferson Ave, S.E., Grand Rapids, Michigan 49503

ISBN 0-8028-0876-X (paper)

Library of Congress Cataloging-in-Publication Data
is available from the Library of Congress

Printed in Great Britain

Reprinted 2002

For Rebecca and Sarah
that they might grow up
to read the four gospels
and love the one Jesus.

In memory of
Iris Joyce Burridge
4th May 1928—1st May 1994
dearly loved and greatly missed.

Contents

Preface and Acknowledgements

'I think you should read the gospels,' my spiritual adviser pronounced, gazing into the roaring log fire as he swirled the golden liquid around his glass. It was a cold Christmas, and we were on retreat at Launde Abbey in the depths of Leicestershire. Uncomprehending, I stared at him; had he finally gone crazy? After all, I had just spent the best part of a decade researching the gospels for my doctorate, and then revising it for publication as an academic monograph!

The next day, out for a brisk walk, I rounded a corner in a quiet valley, and the title, idea and chapter headings for this book fell out of the wintry sky. A couple of years passed, in which nothing much happened about the book— but I did read the gospels. Then, I was fortunate to be awarded some study leave, to teach and lecture in the United States of America, and to research and write this book.

At the end of my leave, away on retreat again (this time 'in the loveable West on a pastoral forehead of Wales,' as Gerard Manley Hopkins wrote of St Beuno's College), I reflected on the different lecture rooms and pulpits, libraries and studies where this material, begun and completed on retreat, had been composed, tested, and refined. Both contexts had been vital—for this book is an attempt to bridge the gap between the prayer cell and the seminar debate. I hope that the scholarly minded will accept the spirituality— for the gospels are not just dead, ancient texts, and that the spiritually inclined will study the scholarship—for God has given us minds. As a symbolic reading of the narrative portraits of Jesus in the four gospels based upon the best of

recent scholarship, I hope it will appeal both to those beginning any form of theological study and also to the thinking
Christian believer. For ease of reading, there are no foot-
notes in the text; annotated suggestions for further reading
are provided at the end of the book. Bible quotations in the
text are taken either from the Revised Standard Version,
New Revised Standard Version, or my own translation from
the Greek.

I am grateful to all those who helped through this period;
I trust the reader will indulge a long list, for many have contributed in various ways. Thanks must begin with Dr David
Harrison, Vice-Chancellor of the University of Exeter and
Chairman of the Lazenby Trust, for granting me study leave
and financial assistance, as well as to the British Academy
for a Personal Research Grant, and for further grants from
the St Luke's Foundation and from the Bishop Philpotts
Trust through the Dean and Chapter of Exeter Cathedral. I
was deeply touched by the warmth and hospitality of all my
American hosts, especially Professor E. Earle Ellis and the
PhD Office of Southwestern Baptist Theological Seminary,
Fort Worth, Texas; Professor Christopher Bryan of the
University of the South, Sewanee, Tennessee, where we kept
a memorable Easter; Professor Daniel Patte and Professor
Mary Ann Tolbert at Vanderbilt University, Nashville;
Professor D. Moody Smith and Dale Martin at the Divinity
School, Duke University, North Carolina; Professor Philip
Stadter and Pat Moyer at the University of North Carolina,
Chapel Hill; Professor Ted Champlin and Professor John
Gages at Princeton University, Professor Beverly Gaventa
at Princeton Theological Seminary and Professor Dan Hardy
at the Center for Theological Inquiry, Princeton; Professor
Leander Keck of Yale Divinity School; Fr Peter Sullivan III
of the Roman Catholic Diocese of Albany, New York; all
the staff and students at General Theological Seminary,
New York for a fascinating month in the Big Apple;
Professor Richard Pervo at Seabury-Western Seminary,
Chicago; and Professor David Aune of Loyola University,
Chicago, for his kindness and continuing interest. I wish to
thank all their colleagues and students who attended my

lectures and seminars for their stimulating contributions and the many conversations, and I remember with profound gratitude all who opened their libraries and studies, rooms and resources, homes and hearts.

Both before and after my leave, I was able to combine the worlds of preaching and scholarship through discussions with my fellow Chaplains at Exeter University, sermons in the University Chapel of the Holy Trinity, and my teaching in the Faculty of Arts. On my return from leave, I was invited to deliver the annual Boundy Memorial Lectures at the University in November 1993, using this material; I am grateful to all who attended for their enthusiasm and responses, which helped to mould the final form of this book. I have been helped by my colleagues in the Department of Theology, especially by Alastair Logan's keen-eyed reading of the typescripts, Ian Markham's endless enthusiasm, and Professor David Catchpole's rigorous scholarship. I wish to thank Ann Newcombe and Sally O'Shea, Chaplaincy and Departmental secretaries, for cheerfully accepting the extra burdens caused both by my leave and this work. I am grateful to Professor Leslie Houlden and my new colleagues at King's College, London, for covering the vacancy in the Dean's Office while I completed this book and my other commitments. I was delighted also to spend some of my leave back at University College, Oxford, for my research at the invitation of the Common Room and my former tutor Dr Christopher Pelling, who started my interest in classical biography so long ago. Jane and Tony Collins, of Collins & Collins Literary Agency, managed to combine our long-standing friendship with professional skill, despite being deluged with typescripts and late-night telephone calls. Philip Law at SPCK provided very helpful encouragement throughout the process. None of this would have been possible without the smiling support of Dr Christopher Southgate, friend and colleague in the Chaplaincy, who bore the pressure of the finals term in my absence; not being a poet myself, I cannot find words to express how much I appreciate his fellowship!

Finally, of course, my own family have not only borne

the brunt of the hours spent away on research or at home in writing, but also provided the love which made it worthwhile. My wife, Susan, has proved the strictest of readers and the most loving of partners; without her, I could do nothing. I enjoyed being at home with my daughters, Rebecca and Sarah, during my leave—and missed them terribly when I was away; their enthusiasm for life and sheer sense of fun provided so much of the energy for the production of this book, and I gladly dedicate it to them.

Oh, and by the way, Gordon, I'm still reading the gospels . . .

Richard A. Burridge
The Feast of the Nativity, December 1993.

Postscript

While this book was in its final stages of production, my mother died suddenly. Her love was ever constant, an intimation of the love of Jesus, while her own mother first taught me to read the gospels. She was proudly looking forward to the publication of this book; may it be a worthy tribute to her memory.

R.A.B.

Four Gospels, One Jesus?

Figure 1 The Four Symbols of the gospels
The Book of Kells, Folio 27V.

1
Four Gospels, . . .

Four portraits

Deep in the heart of the Kent countryside, perched on the side of a gentle hill sloping from the Downs to the flat plain of the Kentish Weald, is a large country house. Chartwell, as it is known, was the country home of Sir Winston Churchill from 1922 until his death. Now belonging to the National Trust, the house reveals much of the man who was Britain's Prime Minister during the dark days of the Second World War. The walls are hung with many photographs and portraits, some of which are his own work as a painter, and some the work of others who attempted to catch, by camera or by brush, something of the character of this great man.

Here is a picture of the statesman in conference with his allies, including President Roosevelt. His face is grim and determined, for the fate of the world rests upon those shoulders. He is dressed soberly, in a dark suit and tie, but he holds a cigar in his right hand. In the background, colleagues, assistants, and secretaries keep a discreet distance, clutching papers. Serious and fateful work is afoot.

Around the corner, another picture: a painting, done by Churchill himself of the very room in which we stand, except that the room was then host to a happy family gathering. It is 'Tea-time at Chartwell, 29 August 1927'. Churchill is casually dressed, smiling at friends and family around the table. It is an ordinary family at tea—and the cares of the world do not obtrude.

Along a corridor we come upon a picture of the man at war: he rides in a camouflaged car, while uniformed men mill all around him. He too wears uniform, for this is an occasion to be 'in with the chaps'. His lips clamp the inevitable cigar in a wide beam as he gives the famous, two fingered 'V for Victory' salute. The men respond with smiles and similar gestures, while overhead fly the war machines to bring about that victory. The mood of all is confident and lifts the heart of the beholder—for so it was intended.

One final, quiet room is adorned with easels and paint pots, and a photograph of Churchill at rest. He sits in a basket chair in the gardens of the Villa Choisi on the shores of Lac Léman in Switzerland. It is August 1946, and he is on holiday, away from the pressures of leading his party in opposition, having lost the previous year's Election; now he relaxes with his painting. His palette is to one side, while he brushes in a gentle picture of trees and water. A white painter's jacket protects his clothes, a trilby is on his head and a cigar in his mouth as he concentrates on his painting, oblivious of the photographer behind him. He is alone and at peace.

Four pictures, all different—each with its own story evoking its own atmosphere and provoking its own response in the viewer—yet all are of one and the same man. This is the skill of the portrait painter, or the clever photographer. Each intends to communicate an image to us and to make us respond. It varies according to the setting, people or objects which are included or excluded, and there is scope for the creativity and inspiration of the artist. So we are introduced to the statesman, the family man, the man of war, or the solitary painter, yet all are recognizably Churchill, and some things (the cigar perhaps) are common to all four pictures. Nevertheless, there are constraints upon the artist and not all images will work equally well: Churchill the monster, with blood dripping from his jaws, killing women and children, for example, would not be recognized—except perhaps as an enemy propaganda cartoon. So, in these simple portraits we have diversity and continuity, inspiration and selectivity, artistic licence within limits.

In today's media age, we know this all too well. We are constantly bombarded by images, from our newspapers to the advertizing hoardings, from the company presentation at work to the commercial TV break at home. The image makers are big business, selling everything from dog food to politicians. Millions are spent on the careful communication of the picture intended—and this is equally true of both people and products. Yet here, too, there are limits to the publicists' creativity: there must be some continuity between reality and image, between the advert and the product, between the person being depicted and the picture being painted. When we put several different portraits of the same person together, we can see immediately both the diversity and the continuity; through comparison we appreciate the skill of the different artists and consider carefully their varying interpretations of the subject. Our appreciation of the person is likely to be enhanced by such study and a fuller, more rounded view of their character will emerge. What we do *not* do is to superimpose the images one on the other, or seek to harmonize them into one single photograph, or reduce them to some simple lowest common denominator.

Yet many Christians treat the portraits of Jesus in the four gospels like this. Tatian, as early as the second century AD, produced the first 'harmony of the four gospels', the *Diatessaron* (Greek for 'through four accounts'). Many Bibles today contain references to build up a similar harmony. Every Christmas, the well-loved passages from the prophets and from the gospels are read together by candlelight to the accompaniment of carols, while Luke's shepherds, Matthew's wise men, and tradition's ox and ass are placed together in the same stable scene. On Good Friday, the various sayings of Jesus from the different gospels' crucifixion scenes are brought together as 'The Seven Words from the Cross' for prayer and meditation; a few days later, all the separate Resurrection stories will be fitted into Luke's chronology of forty days, taken not from his gospel at all, but from the opening chapter of Acts.

Such curious combinations are not unlike attempting to boil down our four images of Churchill, giving him a paint brush in one hand and a victory salute in the other while he wears the top half of his uniform over his casual trousers and comfy slippers to negotiate with Roosevelt at tea time! It is a ridiculous picture which does no justice either to the different photographers or painters, nor to the great subject himself. We know that there is only one Churchill, and that these four portraits each depict his personality in different ways. To appreciate the one person fully, we need the various portraits, considering each in turn with the tools of historical research. Then, and only then, can we hold them together to get a fully rounded understanding of the man, rather than a curious amalgam crashing them into one single picture.

So why do we do this to our four portraits of Jesus? Here, too, an unthinking amalgam of all four does no credit to the genius of the evangelists and can lead to an odd view of Jesus. Once again, we recognize that there is only one person behind these portraits. However, a full understanding of Jesus will be better gained by taking a stroll through the portrait gallery. Here, too, proper study and the use of historical research will lead to a better understanding than an uncritical blending which smoothes out the distinctive picture of each gospel. Admittedly, since Christians revere Jesus in a rather different way from even Churchill's most ardent admirers, some may have anxieties about this process. Therefore, we shall consider shortly the impact of critical tools upon books viewed by many as holy scripture. We will also discuss the relationship of the four portraits to the one person in our final chapter.

Before then, however, we need to expose ourselves to each picture in turn—to spend time in careful, even prayerful, reflection upon what each evangelist is trying to tell us about his understanding of Jesus—and so each gospel will have its own chapter. To prepare us for this task, we should learn something about the tools of the trade, about the different ways we can better appreciate the gospels. Churchill's pictures are better understood in the light of historical analysis and artistic criticism; the same is true of the gospels' portraits of Jesus.

What are the gospels?

First, we need to ascertain what kind of creature we are about to encounter. If we were to treat a cartoon featuring Churchill as though it were a photograph, we would soon make mistakes in its interpretation. Similarly, one does not listen to a fairy story in exactly the same way as to a news broadcast. Correct interpretation of a painting or a story depends on a correct identification of what kind of communication it is, that is, of its *genre*. We differentiate between painting, drama and word, between the spoken word and the written word, between fiction and non-fiction, poetry and prose, tragedy and comedy, legend and history, and so on.

Genre is widely acknowledged as one of the key conventions guiding both the composition and the interpretation of writings. Genre forms a kind of 'contract' or agreement, often unspoken or unwritten, or even unconscious, between an author and a reader, by which the author sets out to write according to a whole set of expectations and conventions, and we agree to read or to interpret the work using the same conventions, giving us an initial idea of what we might expect to find. Thus, TV situational comedies or soap operas are written with certain typical conventions; the viewer recognizes what kind of programme it is and interprets it accordingly. If, however, the viewer is expecting a documentary and interprets it according to the conventions of that genre instead, confusion and mistakes are likely to arise! To avoid such mistakes, we learn to identify genre through a wide range of 'generic features'. These may be in advance, such as a review in the paper, or some publisher's blurb on the book jacket, or advertisement; but generic features are also embedded in the work's formal and structural composition and content. We learn these features through practice, having read similar types of book or watched similar programmes in the past.

As we distinguish between official portraits, family snapshots and political cartoons to appreciate our various pictures of Churchill, before we can read the gospels we have to discover what kind of books they might be. Traditionally, the gospels were viewed as biographies of Jesus. During the nineteenth century, biographies began to explain the character of a great person by considering his or her upbringing, formative years, schooling, psychological development and so on. The gospels began to look unlike such biographies. During the 1920s, scholars like Karl Ludwig Schmidt and Rudolf Bultmann rejected any notion that the gospels were biographies: the gospels appear to have no interest in Jesus' human personality, appearance or character, nor do they tell us anything about the rest of his life, other than his brief public ministry and an extended concentration on his death. The gospels are popular folk literature, collections of stories handed down orally over time. Such an approach became known as 'form criticism' as it concentrated on the 'forms' or 'types' of the individual stories in the gospels. Far from being biographies of Jesus, the gospels were described as 'unique' forms of literature, and this approach dominated gospel studies for the next half century or so.

However, over the last twenty or thirty years, there has been renewed interest in the writers of the gospels as both theologians and as conscious literary artists. This has reopened the question of the genre of the gospels and their place within the context of first century literature. Many genres have been proposed, but increasingly the gospels are again seen as biography. Detailed analysis of many examples of ancient biography and the gospels shows that they share many generic features in common. From the formal or structural perspective, they are written in continuous prose narrative, between 10,000 and 20,000 words in length—the amount on a typical scroll of about ten metres long. Such medium length, single scroll prose works include ancient romance or early novel, historical monographs and biographies. Unlike modern biographies, Graeco-Roman lives do not cover the whole life in strict chronological sequence, complete with detailed psychological analysis of the subject's character. Often, they have only a bare chronological outline, beginning with the birth or arrival on the public scene and ending with the death; the intervening space includes selected stories, anecdotes, speeches and sayings, all displaying something of the subject. Against this background, the gospels' concentration on Jesus' public ministry from his baptism to death does not seem very different.

The content of Graeco-Roman biographies also has similarities with the gospels. They begin with a brief mention of the hero's ancestry, family or city, followed by his birth and an occasional anecdote about his upbringing; usually we move rapidly on to his public début later in life. Accounts of generals, politicians, or statesmen are much more chronologically ordered when recounting their great deeds and virtues, while lives of philosophers, writers, or thinkers tend to be more anecdotal, arranged around collections of material to display their ideas and teachings. While the author may claim to provide information about his subject, often his underlying aims may include apologetic (to defend the subject's memory against others' attacks), polemic (to attack his rivals) or didactic (to teach his followers about him). Similarly, the gospels concentrate on Jesus' teaching and great deeds to explain the faith of the early Christians. As for the climax, the evangelists devote between 15 and 20 per cent of the gospels to the last week of Jesus' life, his death and the resurrection; similar amounts are given over to their subjects' death in biographies by Plutarch, Tacitus, Nepos and Philostratus, since in this crisis the hero reveals his true character, gives his definitive teaching or does his greatest deed. Therefore, marked similarities of form and content can be demonstrated between the gospels and ancient biographies.

Finally, detailed analysis of the verbal structure of the gospels and ancient biographies demonstrates another generic connection. Every sentence in English and in ancient languages must have a subject—the person or object doing the action of the verb. Analysis of the subjects of the verbs can be extended from one sentence to a paragraph and then across a whole work. Most narratives, ancient or modern, have a wide variety of subjects, as different people and objects come to the fore at different times. It is a peculiar characteristic of biography that the attention stays focused on one particular person. Thus, in my analysis elsewhere of ancient biography, I have demonstrated that it is quite common for around a quarter or a third of the verbs to be dominated by *one* person, the hero; furthermore, another characteristic of ancient biography is that another 15 to 30 per cent of the verbs can occur in sayings, speeches or quotations of this person. So, too, in the gospels: Jesus is the subject of a quarter of the verbs in Mark's gospel, with a further fifth spoken by him in his teaching and parables. Matthew and Luke both make Jesus the subject of nearly a fifth of their verbs, while about 40 per cent are spoken by him. About half of John's verbs either have Jesus as the subject or are on his lips. Thus, we can see clearly that, just like other ancient biographies, Jesus' deeds and words are of vital importance for the four evangelists as they paint their different portraits of Jesus.

The gospels, then, are a form of ancient biography. When we study them, we walk through an ancient portrait gallery; the gospels are hung in the same hall as other ancient biographies—and we must study them with the same concentration upon their subject, to see the particular way each author tries to portray his understanding of Jesus. The gospels are Christology in narrative form, or less technically, the story of Jesus. This is why the methods of literary criticism are so vital for gospel studies. We need to learn how they were written, what they contain and how their narratives function. Such methods will help us to listen attentively to the four stories, and to consider each portrait carefully in its own right, just as we might do with Churchill's pictures.

How did the gospels come to be written?   *Sources*

As a schoolteacher, I used to spend long evenings marking children's exercise books. Occasionally, I would suddenly realize that I had seen this answer before, or something very like it, and a frantic search would ensue back through the pile. With the two offending books placed side by side, it could be seen that one child had copied from another—and then the real fun would start, trying to work out, from the style or misunderstandings, who had copied from whom! Now that I teach in a University such experiences are rare, I am glad to say. However, sometimes in one essay I come across a rich vein of material similar to a section already seen in a previous essay, which has been quite different up until now. At the end of this shared paragraph, the essays may diverge again for a page or two, and then, without warning, another overlap occurs. Clearly, neither undergraduate is copying from the other—but how am I to explain the overlapping material? Their reading lists usually show that both students have used the same textbook: perhaps they had it open before them as they wrote, or, more often, they copied details from the textbook into their notes, which were then written up in the essays. Whether this happened consciously or unconsciously (giving them the benefit of the doubt!), such students will still be criticized because of our concepts of truth and accuracy. Plagiarism— the direct copying of one child from another or of a student from a book—is unacceptable in today's world of copyright. Instead, we insist that all sources should be correctly acknowledged and quotations placed in inverted commas with a complete reference.

However, things were different in the ancient world: it is rather difficult to check a reference in a ten-metre handwritten scroll containing no paragraphs or punctuation! In his *Epistle* III.5, Pliny describes the methods used by his uncle when writing his great *Natural History*, which is roughly contemporary with the gospels. Uncle Pliny the Elder has several 'research assistants', educated slaves who read various scrolls for him out loud, while he makes notes on wax tablets to be written up into his text later. The scrolls are so unwieldy that only one could be open on the table before an ancient writer—and this would usually be his principal source. Far from being seen as 'copying' and cheating, this was a compliment to one's predecessor, valuing his work by incorporating it into one's own.

As we must compare the gospels not with *modern* biography but ancient 'lives', so, too, we should not expect today's standards of research to apply to the evangelists; instead, they will use the methods of their own day. Luke faithfully follows ancient literary conventions by mentioning his sources in his 'Preface', 'orderly accounts' already undertaken by 'many', as well as using oral traditions about Jesus handed down from eyewitnesses and early preachers (Lk. 1.1–4). This is typical of ancient writing, and it tells us to expect frequent use of other sources with no further acknowledgment.

In fact, out of 661 verses in Mark's gospel, around 90 per cent occur in Matthew too, and about half are also in Luke. Material occurring in all three gospels is known as the 'triple tradition'; the schoolteacher would immediately assume 'cribbing' and try to work out who is copying from whom. While such notions are not appropriate for ancient sources, we can still ask which came first and who is using the work of the others. As Matthew comes first in the New Testament, it was assumed that it was written first; Augustine described Mark as someone who 'followed him and abbreviated him' (*On the Consensus of the Evangelists*, ii). However, in the last century, literary critical methods suggested that this was unlikely for several reasons. First, the fact that Matthew and Luke include so much of Mark's content and follow his order implies that they both made independent use of his account. Second, Mark's Greek style is rather primitive, full of phrases that sound Aramaic (the language spoken in Palestine at the time of Jesus), while Matthew and Luke 'improve' his Greek when they rewrite his verses into their account. Third, Matthew and Luke both include large amounts of extra material; if Mark used the other two, it is hard to see why he left these sections out. Like our schoolteacher working out the probability of which pupil has copied from which, for such reasons most biblical scholars today still accept 'Markan priority', that is, that Mark wrote first.

Furthermore, two hundred or more remaining verses in Matthew and Luke are found in both—so, is Matthew copying from Luke, or vice versa? This 'double tradition' material comprises mostly Jesus' sayings and parables; in Matthew, it is gathered together into sections, such as the Sermon on the Mount (Matt. 5.1–7.27), while Luke spreads it throughout his gospel. If one is following the other, this difference of order is hard to understand. Also, why should the extra material in one have been left out by the other? Thus, it is unlikely that we have direct copying of one from another, like my school pupils. It is more likely that here we have something analogous to my undergraduates relying independently on the same textbook. Many scholars assume that Matthew and Luke are both using the same source, a collection of Jesus' sayings circulating around the early Christian churches, known as 'Q', from the German word *Quelle*, or 'source'. Since, however, this source has not survived, both its existence and its extent are disputed. Given that only about half of these shared verses have identical verbal overlap, Q may have only included these, if it existed at all; the other hundred or so verses tend to express something similar in different words, and so these may be stories which came to Matthew and Luke independently through oral tradition.

After the triple tradition common to all three gospels, and the double tradition shared by Matthew and Luke, we come to the 'single tradition'—material which occurs only in one gospel. Matthew's unique material includes his stories about Joseph and Jesus' birth, the visit of the wise men, various sections of teaching and some of Jesus' last week and resurrection. Similarly, Luke's own material comprises infancy stories about John the Baptist, Mary's perspective on Jesus' birth, the visit of the shepherds, lots of well-loved parables, and his own description of the crucifixion and resurrection stories. The sources for these are unknown: they may have been stories particularly precious to the evangelists' own churches, or the product of their own research (Lk. 1.1–4), or oral tradition which reached one of them, but not the other.

Finally, we come to the fourth gospel. Traditionally, it was assumed that the writer knew the other three: in the late second century Clement of Alexandria suggested that John wrote a 'spiritual gospel' to supplement the 'physical' facts contained in the others (Eusebius, *Ecclesiastical History* VI.14.7). The actual overlap between John and the others is small, with just less than 10 per cent of their material also appearing in his gospel. The contrast between what is missing from the fourth gospel (e.g. the Transfiguration, exorcisms, parables, the institution of Holy Communion at the Last Supper) and the new sections included (e.g. Nicodemus, Lazarus, the long discourses), leads most scholars to think that this gospel was written quite separately from the other three. Any overlap is best explained by oral traditions about Jesus coming to the evangelist independently.

Therefore the current consensus among gospel scholars about the complex overlapping between the gospels is that Mark wrote first; Matthew and Luke used Mark and another source, 'Q', plus their own material; and that John was written independently of the other three, probably last of all. It may be represented as shown in Figure 2.

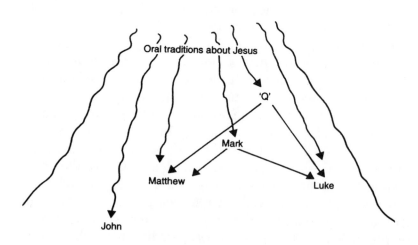

Figure 2   The consensus explanation of the relationships
of the gospels.

Other explanations are possible. Augustine thought that Matthew was first, abbreviated by Mark, and that Luke used them both. In 1776 J. J. Griesbach published the gospels arranged in parallel columns, and suggested that Matthew wrote first, followed by Luke, and lastly Mark abridged the two into his account. Both of these theories have to explain why Mark left out so much of the others—hence the consensus preference for Markan priority. More recently, it has been suggested that Mark wrote first, followed by Matthew, and then Luke used both. This has the merit of doing away with the hypothetical 'Q', since the double material is explained by Luke's use of Matthew; the problem is to explain why Luke should have omitted so much of Matthew, and revised it so extensively.

Since these theories raise more questions than they answer, we shall assume the above consensus view when trying to understand the four portraits of Jesus. If we bear in mind ancient conventions about following sources and their freedom to edit them, rather than modern standards of scholarship, the way each writer handles his source will be revealing.

What sorts of material do the gospels contain? *Forms*

David Watson was a very eloquent and talented speaker who would illustrate his addresses with stories, anecdotes and jokes, using the same material also in his books. I remember listening to him and reading his work when I was a student; often a familiar story would be introduced to make the point. The story would start differently to 'work it in' to the flow of what he was saying, but usually the moral at the end would be the same. So too with his jokes: the setting, or characters, or dialogue might vary according to the need of his audience—but the punch line would be the same. When David died of cancer in 1984, his collection of stories, illustrations, anecdotes and jokes was found neatly catalogued in his study, and some were later published.

Most preachers and teachers, not to mention comedians and entertainers, have similar stores of material. Schmidt and Bultmann noticed that something similar seems to happen in the gospels. Their bulk is comprised of independent little stories of a couple of hundred words each which have been loosely connected to form a narrative. Schmidt pointed to the 'seams' at the start of each story, joining it to the previous one. The story could be 'cut out' from the narrative and stand on its own—hence the technical term for a gospel passage, *pericope*, from the Greek *peri-copto*, meaning to cut around. In fact, this feature of the gospels is well known in the liturgy or Bible readings where we 'cut out' a single gospel story to use in worship or teaching.

The opening chapters of Mark illustrate this. After the start of Jesus' ministry, we find the story of the healing of a leper in 1.40–45: it is introduced simply by, 'a leper came to him . . .', with no indication of place or time. A whole string of separate stories follow, some of which are about healing, but not all; however, they all end with controversy between Jesus and the Jewish leaders, 2.1–12, 13–17, 18–22, 23–28, 3.1–6. Then, in chapter 4, we get another collection, parables about the kingdom of God: the parable of the sower (4.1–9), its interpretation (4.10–20), the lamp and the measure (4.21–25), the growing seed (4.26–29), the mustard seed (4.30–32), concluding with a 'summary' about Jesus' use of parables in 4.33–34. It looks as though Mark pulled out of his cataloguing system a group of *pericopae*, or sections, filed under 'conflict stories' and another lot headed 'parables', and fitted them together.

Thus, 'form critics' like Bultmann and Schmidt analyzed the gospel stories by their *forms*. We immediately distinguish a fairy story from a news bulletin by their openings, 'Once upon a time . . .' and 'Good evening, here is the news . . .', and we expect them to follow different forms: the fairy story involves people and mythical creatures leading up to a happy ending, while the bulletin will have a sequence of separate items, followed by a concluding summary. Similarly, we can classify the various sections of the gospels. There are *miracle stories*, including miracles of nature (e.g. the storm in Mk. 4.35–41) and healings (Mk. 3. 1–6), often with a three-fold form describing the situation, the miracle and the successful result. There are separate *sayings* without any apparent context (e.g. Mk. 2.21–22). There are *parables*, the stories with a point, particularly used by Jesus (e.g. Mk. 4). There are *pronouncement stories*, in which a question or a controversy with the Pharisees leads up to a pronouncement by Jesus—so that v.28 is the punch-line of the pronouncement story in Mk. 2.23–28.

As David Watson would use and re-use stories to illustrate his talks, so these stories were told and re-told by the first Christians in their preaching and teaching. Classifying them like this gives us an insight into the generation between Jesus and the writing of the gospels—the 'oral tunnel'. We can imagine the kind of setting in the life of the early churches where these stories might have been used and the issues which concerned them. John mentions the 'many other signs' which Jesus did which are 'not written in this book' (Jn. 20.30; 21.25). So material was passed around the churches by word of mouth, preaching, teaching and instruction, and considering the 'forms' can help us understand why they were preserved. Since we do not know enough about these early churches, we must beware of circular arguments, deducing the setting from the story and then using the setting to interpret the story! Furthermore, not all the material fits easily into these form categories, and some fit more than one form. However, used carefully, consideration of the forms or types of gospel passage helps us understand the way the stories functioned and were passed on for practical use in the churches, as the early teachers tried to interpret and re-interpret the person and message of Jesus for their congregations, as all preachers have done ever since. These insights will help us look at how the evangelists construct their portraits of Jesus from the stories in their churches and their sources.

What about the authors? *Redaction and composition*

I cannot always read my favourite newspaper at coffee-time in our staff common room, because someone else has bagged it already! Never mind, there are others around, and reading various papers reveals their different styles and views. To spread three or four on the table and to compare their accounts is fascinating (but best not done in the middle of a busy coffee-break!). Although they are all reporting the same story with the same standards of journalism, none the less significant differences can be noted, especially in their coverage of political debate. One paper will always take the government's side, another the opposition's; this editor's views are clearly conservative, while that one espouses liberal causes. Others may be known for their concern for specific issues, such as the environment or racism, and will seek to write things from that angle if possible. Often, these prefer- ences are communicated through very subtle means—the use of a different word here or there, a change in the focus of the story, or the cumulative effect of running several stories over many days or even longer. There is nothing particularly sinister or underhand about this: people know the various papers' interests, and make their choice willingly. Even in reasonably accurate reporting of current events some element of interpretation is inevitable. We recognize how writers build up their interpretation through the way they tell the story.

If this is true for contemporary reporting, it will be even more so for the gospel writers as they interpret the story of Jesus at different times and in different places for their different churches. The stress placed by the form critics on individual gospel passages (*pericopae*) ignores the wider picture of the whole gospel. The evangelists are seen not as authors, but as secretaries, writing down the stories from the oral tradition; they use 'scissors and paste' to stick their work together as it comes, like someone stringing beads on to a necklace haphazardly. In fact, of course, the way an editor pastes up his paper is extremely significant; equally beads can be strung on to necklaces in a variety of ways, not all of which are equally beautiful or communicate the same picture. The whole is more than just the sum of the parts.

During the 1950s and 1960s, another approach to the gospels grew up alongside form criticism, known as *redaction* criticism (from the German, *redaktion*, for news-paper editorial work). If we place three accounts by Mark, Matthew, and Luke of the same story side by side, we can see at once the changes Matthew and Luke have made in their editions of their source, Mark. A 'synopsis' of these three 'Synoptic' gospels arranged in parallel columns is an essential tool for seeing the gospels together (from the Greek *syn*, together, and *opt-*, seeing). Günther Bornkamm's classic essay in 1948, 'The Stilling of the Storm in Matthew', showed that Matthew's account of Jesus' stilling of the storm (Matt. 8.23–27) has reinterpreted Mark's story of a nature miracle (Mk. 4.35–41) into a discipleship lesson about Jesus' ability to save his followers from the storms which rage around them; thus the original story has been made relevant to the life of the early Christian believers (see page 84 below). Such an approach changes everything: now the evangelist is a preacher trying to present his view of Jesus to his hearers, a theologian putting forward his understanding to his readers.

Over the following decades, redaction criticism provided great strides forward in understanding each of the evangelists' portraits of Jesus. It is not enough simply to look at the subtle changes each may have made to their source. We need to look also at the overall picture, the main concerns to which they return regularly, to note their favourite words and phrases, to analyze their vocabulary and images—just as we build up a feel for a newspaper's approach from the words they use, the angle of their reporting or the stories they cover. This book is an exercise in redaction criticism in its attempt to avoid boiling down the four portraits of Jesus into one lowest common denominator, and its concern to look separately at each gospel's interpretation.

Initially, redaction critics helped us to understand the evangelists in their own right by looking at the theological implications of their individual work. However, more recently this method has also demonstrated their skill as literary artists. It is not just the individual emphasis in this or that story which is important. How the author structures a work can be equally revealing; stringing coloured beads in a different order produces a different pattern. *Composition criticism* looks at how the author has composed or ordered his narrative. We have already seen how Mark collected together two groups of stories about conflict (chapter 2) and of parables (chapter 4) to arrange his coverage of Jesus' early activity. Matthew has organized his gospel around five large blocks of Jesus' teaching, the most famous being the Sermon on the Mount. Luke's gospel has a geographical arrangement, from ministry in and around Galilee (4.14–9.50), followed by a long travel narrative as Jesus journeys to Jerusalem (9.51–19.27), to the final section dealing with the events in Jerusalem of Jesus' death and resurrection. John's gospel has a quite different geographical arrangement, with Jesus visiting Jerusalem several times. John's compositional technique links together Jesus' miracles with long discourses explaining their significance, such as the feeding of the 5,000 (Jn. 6.1–14) followed by a discussion on the Bread of Life (Jn. 6.25–59). In arranging their material in this way, the authors are acting like portrait painters, placing their subject with other people or objects to show their interpretation of him. We need to look carefully at the way each evangelist writes, at his use of his sources and also how he presents and orders his material, if we are fully to appreciate all that he is trying to communicate about Jesus.

Literary approaches to the texts   *Narrative and readers*

If the authors of the four gospels are not just preachers and theologians, but also skilled literary artists, then we must use the tools developed in the study of literature throughout our culture. Such literary approaches involve a triangular relationship: the author, the reader and the text operating between them. All too often, gospel studies has stressed only one of these at the expense of the others: if we are to appreciate our four portrait painters, we need to look at the authors themselves, at the way they present their work, and at the response it evokes in ourselves.

The authors of the four gospels are hardly seen in their

own texts: only at the start of Luke (1.1–4) or the end of John (20.30–31; 21.25) do we find personal comment involving 'I'. However, like most ancient biographies, the gospels are written as continuous prose *narrative*; each text, therefore, has a 'narrator', the one who 'tells the story'. Attention to the gospel writers as storytellers is helpful, for in their little asides, observations or comments, their view of Jesus emerges further. Thus, when Matthew uses Mk. 1.32–34 about Jesus' initial healing activity, the narrator points out that 'this was to fulfil' Old Testament prophecy (Matt. 8.17). From frequent similar narrative comments, it is clear that Matthew is keen to stress how Jesus fulfils prophecy as part of his portrait in a way that the other gospel writers were not.

All narratives require a *plot*, a sequence of events which allows the characters and story to develop in a particular way. Central to most plots is *conflict*, which provides move-ment and heightens the tension, leading to a climax of success or failure. All four gospels tell of a growing conflict between Jesus and the religious leaders, and the writers heighten the tension with attempts to find Jesus and his escapes, until we come to the final chapters of his arrest, trial, and death. Each of them narrates this basic conflict with a slightly different plot, again revealing their pictures of Jesus. Plots and characters, events and conflicts need to be narrated in certain *structures*; structuralist approaches to literature point out that the basic structures involve creative tensions between a sender and receiver, subject and object, helper and opponent, and so on. Using these terms, we can see how the evangelists depict Jesus as sent by God to help us, or how he is assisted or opposed in his ministry by those he meets, and, in this way, we build up the evangelists' pictures still further. Because public speaking played such a key role in the ancient world (without TV or mass media), large parts of classical education were devoted to the study of *rhetoric*, the use of language to affect one's hearers in the law courts or public assembly. We should not be surprised, therefore, to find various rhetorical techniques and *literary devices* in the gospels: we will look for repeated literary patterns or motifs, symbols or characters, irony and stylistic structures, settings in time and space, and many, many more. Literary criticism is one of the most exciting and rapidly expanding ways of looking at gospel texts at present.

Having looked briefly at authors and texts, we need to consider the *reader*. When I prepared the initial proposal for this book, my literary agent asked about my intended reader—or to use today's jargon, the 'market'. Every author has an audience in mind, that is, the people to whom the communication is particularly aimed. Ancient literature was often dedicated to a particular reader, usually a wealthy sponsor or patron, addressed directly in a prologue or epilogue. Luke's preface addresses Theophilus by name, using 'you' in the singular, but the book was clearly intended for a wider readership, as I hope this book will be read by more people than just my two daughters to whom it is dedicated! John refers to 'you' in the plural at the end of his book with the intention 'that you may believe' (20.31). We simply do not know who Theophilus was nor the identity of the groups for whom the evangelists wrote. Indeed, although we talk about the 'reader', the primary way for ancient texts to be published was through public readings out loud to a group of listeners; while the educated Roman used this as a means of after-dinner entertainment, the gospels would probably have been read out to congregations in worship.

Authors may write for a specific group, the *intended reader*, while we can find the *implied reader* in the text, the kinds of people they have in mind as they write. Thus Matthew keeps referring to the fulfilment of Jewish prophecy, suggesting that his implied readers are Jewish or familiar with Jewish scriptures; since Luke does not do this, he was probably aiming for a Gentile market. If we are to appreciate the evangelists' different portraits fully, we must understand their implied readers' viewpoint in order to notice the little details which we would miss if we read the gospels through twentieth-century spectacles. Finally, we ourselves are now the *actual readers* of these texts—and they make demands on us. The gospels invite readers to enter their world, to listen to Jesus' words, to watch his great deeds, to appreciate their understanding of him, and to ask ourselves the same questions as the people in the text: 'who is this man?' (Mk. 4.41), or 'what shall I do with Jesus?' (Matt. 27.22). In other words, they are portraits which invite us to respond by joining in the picture. We are not expected simply to admire the artistry, and pass on to view the exhibits in the next room.

Creativity and inspiration   *Criticism of scripture*

Some of our actual readers may be feeling by now that this is all very exciting, but perhaps a bit much! It is usually a good idea in a picture gallery to sit down and take stock occasionally. So far, we have seen that the four gospels are like four portraits of Jesus, and that we need to consider each one carefully to appreciate its particular message. The *genre* of the gospels is ancient biography, because of the large number of generic features they share with Graeco-Roman lives. This fact alone should make us listen attentively to the individual portraits of Jesus, since biography is designed to tell us something about a person. Then we noted the various tools used by scholars: *source criticism*, analyzing the sources of the gospels and which ones used which others; *form criticism*, looking at the different types of individual passages; *redaction criticism*, stressing the evangelists as editors of their material, leading us on to consider them as authors, concerned for the *composition* of their *narrative*; *literary criticism*, with its analysis of the text, plot, structures, rhetorical techniques and the place of the *reader*. These are all helpful aids when standing before the gospels' portraits of Jesus, but we may be excused for feeling a little footsore!

However, some readers may be a little worried about 'criticism': 'How dare we criticize something which millions revere as Holy Scripture?' All these literary tools were forged in the study of secular literature for use on the products of human endeavour, so can they really apply to something believed to be divinely inspired? Also, is the repeated use of words like 'composition' and 'creativity' just a polite way of implying that the gospel writers made it all up? These are genuine concerns sometimes expressed to gospel scholars. While they may be very understandable, such comments presume that the scriptures were dictated by God without any human involvement; the human authors are reduced to mere automata, taken over by God and used simply as writing machines. If this were the case, then words like 'criticism' and 'composition' would indeed be out of place. However, I do not believe that such a view of inspiration is really a Christian understanding. Such notions of automatic writing and possession are more akin to occult practice, and, while ideas of 'divine dictation' are found in some other holy books, they do not occur in the Bible itself.

The New Testament itself might help here. As we have seen, Luke begins with an author's preface, similar to those found throughout classical literature. His reason for writing a gospel is an apparently human decision: having looked at other people's accounts, 'it seemed good to me', or, 'I too decided' to write a book (Lk. 1.3). 2 Peter 1.21 suggests that scriptural prophecy is a combination of human and divine authorship when people 'moved by the Holy Spirit spoke from God' and the word used, *pheromenoi*, implies being lifted or carried, not being driven or compelled, inspiration not domination. Even the famous passage in 2 Timothy 3.16–17 says that 'all scripture is inspired' (*theopneustos*, literally 'God-breathed') for practical relevance: it is useful for teaching, reproof, correction, and training in order to equip Christians for good work. This is exactly what the critical methods suggest that the evangelists have done—to take their material and to interpret it relevantly for their churches or readers. So a scriptural view of scripture implies a combination of human decision and divine inspiration, of perfectly normal literary methods to deliver spiritual teaching. Thus, these critical techniques are required, if we in our generation are to appreciate properly what people 'moved by the Holy Spirit' wrote long ago in a different time and culture.

Furthermore, a classically Trinitarian understanding of

God can help here. If God the Father is the Creator, then he is the source of all creativity; to ascribe creativity to the evangelists does not imply 'making it up', but a creative response to the Creator of all things. If God the Son was incarnate as fully human, without ceasing to be fully divine, then seeing the gospels as the Word of God in human words is comparable; critical analysis of the human composition in the gospels helps us to understand their message. Such tools cannot prove or disprove divine inspiration any more than X-rays or medical inspection of the human body of Jesus could have proved his divinity. Third, if God the Holy Spirit is the giver of life and source of all inspiration, then he was the inspiration of the early Christian prophets, teachers, and preachers bringing the words of the incarnate and risen Jesus to their congregations as well as the inspiration of the evangelists composing their gospels, of the early Fathers confirming the canon of scripture—and even, perhaps, of the humble biblical scholar trying to interpret the person and message of Jesus from the gospels afresh to each generation.

The literary critical approach to the gospels is thus demanded by scripture itself, and by an understanding of God the Holy Trinity: it is a biblical way of reading the Bible, as well as a literary way of reading literature! To sit at the feet of the evangelists and to contemplate their four portraits of Jesus requires all of our skill and faculties— heart and mind, prayer and hard work alike. This is not to deny that there are difficult questions—such as the relationship of the evangelists' portraits to the person of Jesus himself, or about whether all portraits are equally valid— but we will return to these issues in our final chapter, after we have had the chance to use all these techniques to appreciate the four pictures of Jesus in the gospels.

The four living creatures   *The allocation of the symbols*
                                              to the gospels

What are the four portraits of Jesus, and how can we get away from the mixed-up amalgam? A traditional visual aid has been to use the four living creatures found in Ezekiel's vision of God (Ezek. 1.10). In the Cathedral and churches around where I live, these four symbols keep recurring, set in the stone of pulpits, highlighted in stained glass windows, depicted in frescoes, and carved on beautiful wooden ceiling bosses. Often they hold a gospel book, or have the name of one of the evangelists carved below: St Matthew has a human face, St Mark the head of a roaring lion, St Luke a patient-looking ox and St John a sharp-beaked eagle. When I was on study leave in the United States of America to write this book, once again I found them everywhere from the dining hall and chapel of the General Theological Seminary, New York, to the lectern at the University of the South in Sewanee, Tennessee, and in stained glass from the Catholic Cathedral of Albany, capital of New York State, to churches in Vancouver, Canada. So why are they so widespread, and what do they mean?

The origins of these four symbols lie in the visions of the prophet Ezekiel at his call (1.4–28) and of St John the Divine when he saw a door open into the worship of heaven (Rev. 4). In both visions, creatures around the throne of God are described with the four images of a human face, a lion, an ox and an eagle. Ezekiel would have seen statues depicting divine or semi-divine figures in animal form among the Assyrians or Babylonians. They were often identified with the four winds or four compass points, with, for example, Nergal as a winged lion, Marduk as a winged bull, Nebo (or Nabu) as a human being, and Ninib (or Ninurta) as an eagle. None the less, Ezekiel's creatures are servants of God, not gods, and they are human in form (1.5) despite their faces (1.10). Jewish Rabbinic tradition suggests that each creature is chosen for its dignity: the human is the highest of creatures, the lion is king of wild beasts, and the ox chief of domestic beasts, with the eagle as the most exalted of birds; each has dominion in their sphere, yet they are below the throne of God himself (see the midrash on Exod. 15.1, *Rabba Shemoth* 23.13). Lions, oxen and cherubim were on the basin stands in the Temple (1 Kings 7.29) while golden cherubim guarded the ark in the inner sanctuary

(1 Kings 6.23–28), and these images may have inspired Ezekiel's vision as they did that of Isaiah (Is. 6.1–2).

The vision of heaven in Rev. 4 is inspired by many Old Testament visions, including Ezek. 1 in its account of the throne and the four living creatures. Ezekiel has four living creatures, each of which has four faces: a human face in front, a lion's face on the right, the face of an ox on the left, and the face of an eagle at the rear (1.6,10). Rev. 4.7 has four separate creatures in a different sequence—the first 'like a lion', the second 'like an ox', the third 'with a face like a human face', and the fourth 'like a flying eagle'. These four creatures quickly become symbols of the four evangelists in the early church—but there are two main versions: in both the human face is used for Matthew and the ox represents Luke, while John and Mark swap their symbols.

Irenaeus, Bishop of Lyons towards the end of the second century, was a redoubtable defender of the Christian faith. In his great work, *Against the Heresies*, he sets out to correct misunderstandings, and to defend against error. He was well aware that the multiplicity of gospels could be used to suggest that no single gospel was perfect. He argues that there had to be *four* gospels, not more nor fewer, because of the four zones or compass points of the world, the four winds, the four cherubim and the four covenants (Adam, Noah, Moses, Christ—*Against the Heresies*, III.11.8–9). While we might not find this kind of argument convincing today, it clearly went down a storm in the second century! He says that the four faces are 'images of the disposition of the Son of God' and allocates the human face to Matthew, the lion to John, the ox to Luke, and, finally, the eagle is Mark. How did this version come about?

We have already seen that each gospel is about the length of a single parchment scroll. Although two might have been squeezed on to a scroll with very small writing, four would never have fitted. A collection of four gospels requires the development in the second century of the *codex*, a book comprised of separate sheets or pages, bound or tied together. The four gospels are put together in this way around AD

150–180, and there are two main traditions for the *order* of the four. The order *Matthew–John–Luke–Mark* is known as the 'Old Latin' or 'Western' order because of its frequency in early Latin manuscripts and its use among writers and churches in the western Mediterranean. It probably resulted from giving the two apostles priority (Matthew–John), followed by the two apostolic associates in order of length (Luke–Mark). As Bishop of Lyons, in southern France, Irenaeus would have used this Western order, and his allocation of the symbols results from applying Ezekiel's sequence to it, thus:

human	*lion*	*ox*	*eagle*	= Ezekiel 1.10
Matthew	*John*	*Luke*	*Mark*	= Old Latin or Western order

So, the use of the four symbols for the gospels is very early indeed. The original version of Victorinus of Pettau's Commentary on Revelation (*c.* AD 300) also used this allocation. Finally, Ambrose, Bishop of Milan around AD 390, applies the symbols to the evangelists in the Western order with John as the lion and Mark as the eagle (see Ambrose's *Exposition on Luke*, Prologue, 7–8).

However, this was not the only version. The order of the gospels we know in our Bibles—*Matthew–Mark–Luke–John*—first appears in a fragment known as the Muratorian Canon, dating around AD 170–200. This order tends to be used in Greek writers in the eastern Mediterranean. Theophilus, a contemporary of Irenaeus, wrote a Commentary on the four gospels in which he suggests that the lion represents Mark, while the eagle is for John; Matthew and Luke are agreed as the human face and the ox. This results from applying the sequence of Ezekiel 1.10 to the order used in the east—and Antioch, where Theophilus was Bishop, was in Syria:

human	*lion*	*ox*	*eagle*	= Ezekiel 1.10
Matthew	*Mark*	*Luke*	*John*	= Greek or Canonical order

These were the two main allocations (alternating Mark and

John) based upon the two different orders of the gospels used at different ends of the Mediterranean about AD 200. Other minor versions do appear infrequently (e.g. in Augustine of Hippo). However, Jerome tidies things up and standardizes the Canonical order of the gospels across the ancient world through his Latin translation of the New Testament, the Vulgate, around AD 400. He also uses the second allocation of the symbols above (namely, Matthew = human, Mark = lion, Luke = ox, and John = eagle) in his Commentary on Ezekiel and the Preface to his Commentary on Matthew. This then becomes the dominant version.

The four symbols as visual teaching aids
Reasons and explanations

Clearly, the allocation of the symbols resulted from applying Ezekiel to one's customary order of the gospels—and the explanations followed on later, some of which are rather strained. The reasons given are all derived from the opening verses of each gospel. We saw previously that, in the absence of modern book jackets and publicity blurbs, texts in the ancient world were often known by their opening word(s), and their literary genre could be recognized from the opening paragraph, preface or prologue. Thus, the symbols are applied to the opening verses of each gospel, the first to be encountered by the reader. Most ancient commentators agree that Matthew is represented by the human face, because he begins with the human genealogy of Jesus, Matt. 1.1–17. After his preface, Luke mentions the priestly office of Zechariah (Lk. 1.5f); since the ox in the Old Testament was a sacrificial animal for priests, the Fathers quickly linked Ezekiel's third face, the ox, to the opening of the third gospel.

Irenaeus looked at the openings of John and Mark for the lion and eagle. He saw the sovereign character of the lion in John's prologue about the Word being with God (1.1–18). The eagle is the spirit of prophetic inspiration—and Mark begins with the prophecy of Isaiah in 1.2–3; the eagle also explains why Mark's account runs along concisely.

Victorinus tried to improve on this: John proclaims the divinity of Christ right at the start of his gospel, 'like a lion roaring', while Mark is the eagle because he makes a flying start to his gospel! While Mark does go straight into his account with no prologue or birth narratives, things are getting a bit desperate here as the Fathers impose the Western order of the gospels on to Ezekiel's sequence and find reasons for the allocation afterwards. Over the years, the explanation for Matthew stays the same—the human genealogy. In addition to the priesthood of Zechariah, Luke's account of Jesus' sacrificial death is compared with an ox. Ambrose pointed to the reference about the death of the fatted calf in the parable of the prodigal son (Lk. 15.23) as another reason for the ox symbol; he also sees Mark's eagle as a sign of the risen and ascended Christ.

Jerome keeps the same reasons for Matthew (genealogy = human face) and Luke (priesthood = ox). However, Mark now has to become the lion: since lions roar in deserted places (Psalm 104.21; Amos 3.4), and Mark begins with the 'voice crying in the wilderness' (1.3), that solves that problem. The lion is a symbol of the (loud?) preaching of John the Baptist in the desert to prepare the way for Jesus at the start of Mark. John, now the fourth gospel, is the eagle, 'hurrying to the heights borne aloft on eagle's wings' to proclaim Jesus as the Word of God.

Whatever we might think today about such reasoning, in a semi-literate age visual symbols were vitally important for teaching. These four pictures stood for the gospels and each was recognized by its symbol right at the start without the need for reading. Equally, this imagery was used for summaries of the gospel message, that Jesus was born as a man, sacrificed like an ox, rose again triumphant like a lion, and ascended like an eagle, extending his wings to protect his people. For these reasons, we can easily understand how these four symbols came to dominate early Christian art.

From Jerome to the *Book of Kells*   *The illuminated gospels*

Jerome's translation quickly became the 'Vulgate', which means 'Common' version. The canonical order of *Matthew–Mark–Luke–John* applied to Ezekiel's sequence was fairly standard and the four symbols can be found in frescoes, mosaics, pulpits, crosses and so forth from the fourth century onwards. Christianity arrived in Britain by about AD 200; rooms in Roman villas were turned into Christian chapels, and British bishops took part in the great Councils of the church. The faith spread through the Province and beyond through the ministry of great saints like David and Patrick. After the departure of the Roman legions around AD 410, the Christian churches continued independently, especially in Ireland, Scotland and northern England, giving rise to the Celtic Christian tradition.

When Pope Gregory sent St Augustine as the first Archbishop of Canterbury on his mission to Kent in 595/6, he equipped him with 'lots of books', including the gospels and the New Testament in the Vulgate version. A sixth-century Italian gospel manuscript (now in the library of Corpus Christi College, Cambridge, MS 286) is traditionally thought to be one of these books—hence it is called *St Augustine's Gospels*. When Pope John Paul came to visit Canterbury Cathedral on 29 May 1982, this manuscript was placed on the throne of St Augustine. Although the gospels are not completely preserved, one illustrated page depicts Luke holding his gospel in one hand and stroking his beard thoughtfully with the other, while above him there is a beautifully drawn winged ox (folio 129v). Thus the habit of illustrating gospel books with the symbols of the evangelists may have come to the British Isles with St Augustine himself.

However, it was Celtic craftsmen who produced the most exquisite examples. The *Book of Durrow* (now in Trinity College, Dublin, MS A.4.5) was probably produced around AD 650–675 in Northumbria or Iona. It begins with a full page illustration of the evangelists' symbols arranged around a cross, but the order is immediately striking—human, eagle, ox and lion; also, the full page animal introducing Mark is an eagle. In other words, the artist is still following the old Western order for the symbols, as in Irenaeus and Ambrose. The Synod of Whitby in AD 664 brought the Celtic churches into line with the Roman churches of the Mediterranean over things like the date of Easter, and the use of the Vulgate translation and order of the New Testament. It is interesting to note that this artist, working on the *Book of Durrow* at that very time, harks back to pre-Roman influence by giving Mark the eagle and John the lion. Perhaps the symbols are being used here as a last Celtic protest?

However, this is the last time we see this allocation of the symbols. The actual depictions of the symbols can vary: the *Echternach* gospels (*c.* AD 698, now in the Bibliothèque Nationale in Paris, MS lat. 9389) has a rather stylized man for Matthew, a fierce rampant lion for Mark, an ox quietly plodding across the page for Luke, and an eagle with folded wings for John, more reminiscent of a pigeon than someone hastening to the heights of heaven! By way of contrast, the eagle in the *Corpus Christi gospels* (MS 197B) is very fierce, with a hooked beak and splayed talons. Does this tell us anything about how each scribe viewed the different gospels?

The *Lindisfarne gospels* (in the British Library, Cotton MS Nero D.IV) combine the symbols with the portraits of the evangelists. As Figures 3, 5, 6 and 7 show, in each case, the gospel writer is seated with his pen and book (the Synoptists are still writing theirs, but John has rather smugly finished his!), but his symbol hovers overhead, clutching another book, presumably acting as the inspiration for the text. Two of the four animals—the ox and eagle—bear a remarkable resemblance to the evangelists' symbols carved on the coffin of St Cuthbert, who died in 687. Perhaps these gospels were written in honour of Cuthbert for the enshrining of his coffin sometime between 687 and 698.

Iona may have been the production site for our final, and crowning, example. Manuscript A.1.6 in Trinity College, Dublin is better known as the *Book of Kells*, after the monastery in central Ireland where it spent most of the Middle Ages. St Columba's shrine and relics were moved to Kells in 878 from Iona where they were at risk from Viking attack, and it is quite possible that this gospel-book came to Kells with them. They may have been produced for the enshrining of St Columba at Iona, around AD 750. Here the symbols run riot. There are several pages where all four are brought together (see Figure 1 above), and they feature regularly in their respective gospels, as well as in the 'canon-tables'—a cross-referencing system for looking at similar passages in different gospels by listing sequences of numbers referring to the various passages. The distinctive images are haunting and immediately recognizable, and they are often used today to illustrate Commentaries or books about the gospels. In subsequent centuries and on into the mediaeval period, it became common to decorate the outside cover or first page of gospel books with the four symbols arranged around a central figure of Christ (as on the twelfth-century Psalter from Westminster Abbey in Figure 9 page 162 below)—truly an impression of four gospels, one Jesus.

Our four portraits of Churchill were each set in a different room, and reflected the atmosphere of that room—the military leader, the relaxed painter, the statesman, the family man, and so on. So, too, for our portraits of Jesus. These symbols began with a prophetic vision of God and were used to interpret the written gospels in non-literary cultures; as we move increasingly into a visual culture today, these simple images might again help us to understand the four gospels. Instead of using them for each evangelist, we shall follow Irenaeus (*Against the Heresies*, III.11.8–9) and apply them to 'the disposition of the Son of God'—the four portraits of Jesus—in an attempt to understand the 'narrative Christology' of each 'biography' separately. In each case, we shall be looking at the gospel through the picture of Jesus painted by that evangelist, and we may treat it like a room, walking around it and pondering all it contains. We shall consider particularly the beginning and end of each gospel, the accounts of Jesus' birth or arrival, and his death and resurrection. We shall notice how the book has been arranged, as well as the distinctive emphases of plot and characterization each writer has given to his portrait in order to make use of the hermeneutical key of seeing the gospels as biographies of Jesus. My hope and my prayer is that, because of the visual impact of these symbols, they may help us to clarify each of the four Christologies, to change our perceptions away from the unthinking harmonized amalgam to the four gospel portraits of the one Jesus.

2
The Roar of the Lion— Mark's Jesus

The lion's appearance   *Symbolism and meaning*

The opening of any ancient biography usually tried to say something about who the subject was and where he came from. Often the first words included the subject's name, and, perhaps, a brief comment about his family, ancestry or home town. Unlike modern biography, however, there was no need to cover the birth, all the early life, and education in great detail. Often, the narrative moved swiftly through several decades to the subject's arrival on the public scene.

Mark's opening is uncompromising and direct: 'The beginning of the gospel (good news) of Jesus Christ, the Son of God.' (Mk. 1.1) Who is this person and where does he come from? We are not told—just the subject's name, as in many ancient Lives. Mark may give us some information in the titles for Jesus: 'Christ' is the Greek translation of the Hebrew 'Messiah', someone who 'has been anointed'. While Paul's letters use 'Christ' as almost a surname for Jesus (as here), elsewhere Mark uses it as a title, 'the Christ' (e.g. 8.29; 14.61; 15.32). Furthermore, the phrase 'the Son of God' is missing in some ancient manuscripts; modern editors disagree whether it was in Mark's original. So, we begin simply with the name of Jesus: there are no birth stories, no mention of Bethlehem, and no genealogy or Davidic ancestry. Mark does not have time for these preliminaries. Jesus just arrives fully grown, of indeterminate age, from Nazareth to be baptized by John in the Jordan (1.9). One is reminded of Aslan, the great lion in the *Narnia*

Figure 3 St Mark, *Lindisfarne Gospels,* Folio 93b.

Chronicles of C. S. Lewis, who suddenly appears from over the sea without warning but exactly when he is needed: 'Aslan was among them though no one had seen him coming.' (C. S. Lewis, *The Horse and His Boy*, Puffin/Penguin, 1965, p. 182).

Thus we come to the lion symbol for St Mark. Since the Fathers usually link the symbols to the opening of each gospel, the lion is a symbol of John the Baptist, the 'voice crying in the wilderness'. Others suggest that the lion, as king of the beasts, represents Jesus' royal power in Mark. While the lion is often seen as kingly in other Ancient Near Eastern cultures, this is not the main image in the Bible. The earthy wisdom of Proverbs compares the roar of a lion to a king's anger (19.12; 20.2), and even to a wicked ruler (28.15; see also Zeph. 3.3). More commonly, the lion is seen as a predator suddenly appearing out of the forest to attack flocks (1 Sam. 17.34–7) or human beings (1 Kings 13.24–26); the Psalmist uses lions as symbols of his enemies (Pss. 17.12; 22.13). When the prophets liken God to a lion, it is as a symbol of judgement and destruction, rather than royalty (Jer. 49.19; 50.44; Hosea 13.7–8), and a cause of lamentation (Lam. 3.10). The lion is thus an uncomfortable image in the Bible and not the most obvious choice for 'Gentle Jesus, meek and mild'! However, let us see what happens if we read Mark's story with the image of Jesus as a lion before us. After all, we are often told that 'Aslan is not a tame lion'—even if, surprisingly, that exact phrase never occurs in C. S. Lewis' books!

The bounding lion   *Mark's style, structure and narrative technique*

Whenever Aslan does appear in the Narnia stories, he dashes from place to place as he is needed in great leaps and bounds: 'he rushes on and on, never missing his footing, never hesitating' (*The Lion, the Witch and the Wardrobe*, Puffin/Penguin, 1959, p. 150). So too in Mark's first chapter. The opening stories concern John the Baptist's ministry and preaching (1.4–8) and the baptism of Jesus

(1.9–11), both substantially briefer than Matthew or Luke's account. Then we have a brief mention of temptation (1.12–13) with no narrative—although there is the interesting note, unique to Mark that Jesus was 'with the wild beasts'! Then, lion-like, Jesus bounds off into his work—proclaiming the kingdom of God and repentance (1.14–15), forming a group of disciples (1.16–20) and engaging in a teaching and healing ministry, the man with an unclean spirit in the synagogue (1.21–28), Peter's mother-in-law (1.29–31), many others who are sick or possessed (1.32–34), going round the towns and synagogues of Galilee (1.35–39) and healing a leper (1.40–45). The sheer pace of it all is unrelenting. This material occupies several chapters in Matthew and Luke, but here Jesus rushes around just like a bounding lion. It all happens 'and immediately', 'at once' or 'straight away', which are all translations of *kai euthus*, which occurs 11 times in chapter 1 alone (vv. 10, 12, 18, 20, 21, 23, 28, 29, 30, 42, 43), and is linked with 'make his paths straight' (*eutheias*, 1.3). No wonder he had to get up very early to pray in v.35! This pace continues, with *euthus* occurring over 40 times in Mark, about as often as the rest of the New Testament put together.

Pace and vividness are also imparted by Mark's predilection for the use of the 'historic present', dropping into the vivid present tense when narrating a story in past time. After the past narrative of John the Baptist and Jesus' baptism in 1.4–11, the Greek of v.12 changes into the present for 'immediately the Spirit *drives* him out into the wilderness' before returning to past verbs for the rest of that story; similarly, 'they entered' Peter's house where his mother-in-law 'was lying' in bed, but 'immediately they *tell* him about her' (1.30). Occasionally this can help bring any story suddenly alive, but Mark does it 151 times in his gospel, which perhaps is a trifle excessive! This is why many English versions do not translate these as present tenses, remaining in past time. Unfortunately this means that we miss Mark's vividness and pace: no one knows where the lion comes from, or where he is going as he leaps on.

This sense of urgency can also be seen in Mark's use of

time. While Luke carefully anchors his account in Roman and Jewish civil and religious dates (Lk. 3.1–2) and John implies a ministry of a couple of years (with three Passovers in Jn. 2.13; 6.4; 12.1/13.1), for Mark the time is always now and things are urgent. Apart from the forty days in the wilderness (1.13), his account could be fitted into one month, including the gap of 'six days' in 9.2. Mark tends to describe a busy day in some detail, with episode following episode 'immediately', followed by vague and general summaries indicating a lapse of time for similar teaching or healing: for example, 'he went throughout Galilee, proclaiming the message in their synagogues and casting out demons' (1.39) presumably does not mean that Jesus did this all on the same day!

The majority of the 'immediately's' occur during the first half of the gospel, which helps to build up this impression of a fast-moving ministry. Mark's gospel is structured around Peter's confession of Jesus as Messiah, marking the turning point at 8.27–30. There are paragraphs acting as a kind of 'hinge' linking the major sections (like 1.14–15 after the beginning or 8.22–26 at the mid-point). The gospel was designed to be read out loud, rather than for detailed written analysis and these links prepare the listener for the change of gear. It is like a symphony's initial flurry of violins scurrying around in chapter 1 with this pace continuing through the first movement set in Galilee for Jesus' ministry of healing and exorcism, proclaiming the kingdom and achieving some success up to 8.26. Then things change to a more leisurely pace for the middle section as Jesus' identity and destiny become clearer *en route* to Jerusalem under the lengthening shadow of the Cross, 8.27–10.52. The third movement balances the first by picking up the pace again to describe only one week, the last days set in Jerusalem, with no exorcisms or healing and the kingdom theme changing into the Cross and Passion. It is as though the lion rushes around at first, pauses to regain his strength and then moves purposefully ahead to the kill—and we shall follow this pattern below.

However, the pace of the opening chapter must not blind

us to Mark's narrative artistry. Like a good storyteller, he grabs our attention through these fast-moving cameos—but subtly introduces many of his important themes, like a composer sketching out the major motifs for his symphony. We begin with Jesus' baptism in 1.9–11. The next time baptism appears, Jesus uses it as a metaphor for his death, asking James and John if they can 'be baptized with the baptism that I am to be baptized with' (10.38–39). Furthermore, in Mark's account the heavens are 'torn apart' (*schizo* in Greek, giving us *schism*), unlike the milder 'opened' (*anoigo*) in Matthew (3.16) and Luke (3.21); the only other time Mark uses this word is when the curtain of the Temple is 'torn apart' at Jesus' death in 15.38. Significantly, the tearing of the heavens is followed by a voice from heaven saying that Jesus is 'my beloved Son' (1.11); the tearing of the Temple veil leads into the declaration by the centurion, 'Truly, this man was the Son of God' (15.39). Despite its brevity and pace, the opening scene is linked to the final scene fifteen chapters later: like a pair of bookends, the baptism and the crucifixion mark the 'beginning of the good news of Jesus' (1.1), and his end. Jesus appears suddenly, from nowhere, to be baptized—and he is baptized in order to die.

If Mark's overture suggests that the cross will be the major thread, it also tries out secondary themes. Jesus' identity is declared by the voice from heaven; as the Son of God, he engages in preaching, teaching and healing for the rest of this chapter—and these will be his main activities as the story progresses. However, he also encounters conflict at both the supernatural level in the wilderness (1.12–13), and from human beings, who are amazed and question his authority (1.27). He calls disciples (1.16–20), yet forbids both demons and humans to declare his identity (1.34; 44). These are all motifs which will recur regularly as events unfold.

Finally, we need to consider Mark's style and narrative techniques as he builds up his portrait of Jesus. Mark used to be criticized for his poor Greek and bad style; more recently, commentators have noted the way in which his manner of writing reflects the directness of his account. It is unlikely that Greek was his first language: usually, Greek prose narrative flows along with each section connected carefully together. Mark links no less than eighty-eight sections of his gospel with the simple word 'and'; the technical literary term for this is *parataxis*. A further nineteen sections have no link at all, and this is called *asyndeton*, 'unlinked'. While both of these stylistic features betray Semitic influence, suggesting that Mark is thinking in Aramaic, none the less they move the story quickly on and build up the pace. Mark's style is brief and terse, preferring concrete action to abstract discourse; it is colloquial, designed for easy listening rather than for the close attention required by a written text. As in much spoken material, Mark frequently combines related nouns and verbs (*pleonasm*) to get the point across: see for example the repetition of teach-taught-teaching in 1.21–22 or 4.1–2—no one can fail to recognize Jesus as teacher. The lion does not deliver polished oratory: he roars—and the message is clear!

One narrative technique worth noting is the so-called Markan 'sandwich' where one story provides the 'filling' between two pieces of 'bread'. Thus, the accusation that Jesus is empowered by Satan (3.22–30) is sandwiched between the unbelief of his own family (3.20–21 and 31–35). Similarly, Jesus' cursing and the subsequent barrenness of the fig tree surround his clearing out of the Temple, implying that it too is cursed and barren (11.12–20); the woman's loving response in anointing Jesus is contrasted with the plotting taking place around it (14.1–11). In each case, the story on the inside illuminates the surrounding narrative, by way of commentary, comparison or contrast. Other sandwiches include 5.21–43, 6.6–30 and 14.54–72.

In the sandwich the third element repeats the first, giving a 1-2-1 formation. Elsewhere, Mark forms groups of three, developing the intensity or development, 1-2-3, in case the listener missed the point the first time. Thus, we have three boat scenes with the disciples (4.35–41; 6.45–52; 8.14–21) where Luke only has the first one, and Matthew leaves out the boat in the third one; either the later evangelists do not share Mark's enthusiasm for three, or Mark is making a point about how slowly the disciples catch on! The three Passion predictions become progressively more detailed (8.31; 9.31; 10.32–34). The three commands to 'keep awake and watch' in 13.33–37 are matched by the tired disciples' three sleeps in Gethsemane (14.37, 40, 41). In the Passion, Peter denies Jesus three times, building in vehemence in 14.66–72; Pilate asks the crowd three questions in 15.9, 12, and 14; and there are three time references at three hourly intervals when Jesus is on the Cross, the third (15.25), sixth (15.33) and ninth hours (15.34). This threefold pattern is not coincidence; it is all part of Mark's careful building up of the pace and sequence of his story of Jesus.

So, through all these features—the opening rush, the frequent use of 'and immediately', the compression of time and use of present tenses, the careful structure, the simple style with its sandwiches and three-fold patterns—Mark conveys a clear impression of Jesus' pace, and the urgency of his task. No bounding lion ever moved so quickly, and, like Aslan, none may delay him:

> 'Lucy said crossly, "Wait a minute." "Daughter of Eve," said Aslan in a graver voice, "others also are at the point of death." . . . and for the next half an hour they were busy.' (C. S. Lewis, *The Lion, the Witch and the Wardrobe*, Penguin, 1959, p. 163).

The beast of conflict   *Opposition and ministry, Mark 1–8*

One thing is clear about lions in every age and culture: they are powerful fighters with a keen sense of territory. After the opening flurry of chapter 1, Jesus starts to roam far and wide around the northern territories by the sea of Galilee: Capernaum (1.21; 2.1); Galilee itself (1.39); the Greek territory of the Gerasenes and the Decapolis (5.1, 20; 7.31); Nazareth (6.1); Gennesaret (6.53); Tyre and Sidon (7.24, 31); Dalmanutha (8.10); Bethsaida (8.22); Caesarea Philippi (8.27), Galilee and Capernaum again (9.30, 33) before eventually heading south for Judea and the road to Jerusalem (10.1, 32). There are about forty scene changes while he roams up and down the land: mountains and deserts, grainfields and pasture-land, the river and the sea, boats and synagogues, publicly outdoors and within private houses. Thus, we can add a sense of _space_ to the _pace_ already noted: not only does the lion bound around with urgency because the time is short, but also he covers huge tracts of land, crossing and recrossing ground, seeking out those who need him, and roaring his message.

This major section from 1.16 to 8.26 is taken up with accounts of Jesus' ministry through his teaching and his miracles. Both activities immediately raise the question of his authority: he teaches as one with authority (1.22), while the obedience of unclean spirits to his authority amazes the crowd (1.27). However, right at the start his teaching and miracles lead to a conflict of authority with the religious leaders (2.10).

Mark stresses Jesus as teacher in the repeated noun-verb combinations in 1.21–22 and 4.1–2, and in his little 'summary' passages (e.g. 1.14; 1.39; 4.1; 6.6; 6.34). Jesus is regularly addressed as 'Teacher' both by his disciples (4.38) and those who seek his help (5.35; 9.17). Mark preserves the use of the Jewish term 'Rabbi' by Peter (9.5; 11.21) and by Judas at the moment of betrayal (14.45). Surprisingly, however, little actual teaching is recorded here. We have really only four parables: the sower (4.1–20), the seed growing secretly (4.26–29—occurring only in Mark), the mustard seed (4.30–32) and the tenants of the vineyard (12.1–12). On the other hand, the sheer mass of teaching material in Matthew and Luke—both parables and sections of direct teaching—is probably derived from their shared 'Sayings' source, Q (see pages 10–12 above). While Q seems to have had no narrative, Mark is the opposite—lots of narrative, but little teaching. Any direct teaching given by Jesus emerges in dialogue with the religious leaders in response to their questions (2.15–28, 3.23–30 and 7.1–23). There is no systematic account of Jesus' teaching in Mark, despite calling him 'Teacher'. Mark's Jesus is a creature of action.

In contrast to his few parables, Mark contains seventeen

miracles, which, allowing for his shorter length, is proportionally more than any other gospel. They include exorcisms (1.23–26; 5.1-20), healings (1.30–31, 40–44; 2.1–12; 3.1–5; 5.22–34, 35–43; 7.25–30, 32–37; 8.22–26), and power over nature itself (4.36–41; 6.35–44, 47–51; 8.1–9). The vast majority take place in this first half of the gospel, with only the exorcism of the epileptic boy (9.14–29), and the granting of sight to Bartimaeus (10.46–52) taking place after the turning point. In addition, the first half also includes summary statements about Jesus' regular ministry of healing and exorcism (1.32–34; 1.39; 3.10–12; 6.5; 6.55–56). Mark's terminology gives us a clue: unlike John or Luke, he never describes Jesus' acts as 'signs' or 'wonders'. Only the Pharisees and 'this generation' seek signs (8.11–13); it is false Christs who perform signs and wonders to lead the elect astray (13.22). Instead, Mark prefers the term *dunamis* for Jesus' miracles (6.2, 5, 14), 'mighty acts' of power—literally, dynamite! The lion is indeed an appropriate symbol for Mark's Jesus: these powerful acts are carried out by a powerful creature—but they lead him into conflict.

This is best exemplified in Mk. 3.19b–35: It begins with Jesus going *'eis oikon'* after choosing his disciples. This phrase can mean 'into a house', but because his family soon appear, it probably means that 'he went home'. The enthusiasm of the crowd even prevents Jesus from taking a meal break (v.20), a contrast to the hostile reactions which follow. For now his family appear, to restrain him because they believe Jesus to be mad (v.21). Then the story is interrupted by the scribes accusing Jesus of being possessed by the devil, and Jesus' response, describing the cosmic conflict in graphic terms (vv.22–30). Finally, his mother and brothers get a message to him through the crowd (vv.31–32). Rather than going to see them, Jesus curtly dismisses their claim upon him: 'whoever does the will of God is my brother and sister and mother' (vv.33–35).

This is a typical Markan 'sandwich', the 1-2-1 formation discussed above. He is implying a link between the different reactions from the crowd, the family, and the scribes. Furthermore, Jesus' family oppose him just as much as the authorities—and they are all caught up in the cosmic conflict with Satan and risking blasphemy against the Holy Spirit (v.29). Strong stuff, indeed! It is *too* strong for Matthew and Luke: they dismantle Mark's 1-2-1 formation and link the central section describing Jesus' argument with the scribes about Beelzebul with other material about seeking signs and unclean spirits (Matt. 12.22–45; Lk. 11.14–32, presumably from Q). Both Matthew and Luke completely omit from their gospels Mark's opening section about Jesus' family considering him mad (Mk. 3.20–21); since very few of Mark's verses are omitted by them both in this way, this indicates clearly how Matthew and Luke find this idea too hard to stomach. Matthew does have Mark's final section about Jesus rejecting the family's request at the end of his controversy section (Matt. 12.46–50), but Luke moves it to several chapters earlier, where it is unconnected with anything else (Lk. 8.19–21).

Matthew and Luke both begin their gospels with stories about Jesus' family and his birth; Mark does not—Jesus bounds on to the stage like a lion, fully grown. Matthew and Luke tone down the conflict between Jesus and his family; Mark deliberately links it to the other opposition to Jesus from the authorities and the cosmic battle with Satan. When the lion cub is fully grown, he has to leave his family, probably after a tussle or two, and go off to form his own pride.

Conflict is central to most good stories; it provides the power and tension to the narrative as the hero overcomes his difficulties to reach his goal or win his prize. The final resolution of the conflict usually forms the climax of the story. Mark's Jesus is a powerful figure who bounds on to the stage and declares that the moment is NOW! As Jesus roams the length and breadth of the northern territories, Mark gradually charts the build up of his battle with all that opposes him, which will lead to the climax on a cross in Jerusalem. Unlike Matthew and Luke, he is not afraid to show the conflict beginning even within Jesus' own family. It spreads to his home town, where his former friends and neighbours' lack of faith means that Jesus '*could* do no powerful act there' (Mk. 6.1–6; compare Matthew's lighter, 'Jesus *did* not do many mighty works there', Matt.13.58).

The conflict with the authorities began when they questioned Jesus' authority to forgive the paralytic (2.6–8). Mark then strings a number of conflict stories together about Jesus' choice of sinners as followers and his activity on the sabbath, until he provokes the Pharisees and Herodians, not normally known for being allies, to conspire together against him (2.13–3.6). From then on we have various references to their hidden plots (3.6; 11.18; 12.12; 14.1–2) and their open arguments with Jesus (7.1–15; 8.11–15; 10.1–12; 11.27–33; 12.13–40).

However, the centrepiece of Mark's 1-2-1 formation of 3.19b–35 reveals that the true conflict is greater than family or human authorities: it is with the devil himself. It is hard to imagine a more graphic image of conflict than Jesus likening himself to a burglar entering a strong man's house to tie him up and plunder his property (3.27). The conflict with Satan begins in the desert, where, instead of Matthew and Luke's debates about Jesus' identity, Mark tersely states that he was 'tested by Satan'; non-human elements are emphasized by the wild beasts and angels (1.13). This dimension rapidly confronts Jesus in the synagogue, where one unclean spirit speaks for them all, 'What have you to do with *us*, Jesus of Nazareth? Have you come to destroy *us*?' (1.23–27). Jesus' power is shown as this spirit obeys him (1.27), and by various summaries of his exorcisms (1.32–34, 39; 3.11, 22). A legion of demons is cast out and drowned in the Gerasenes' pigs (5.1–20) and Jesus shares this conflict and his authority with his disciples (6.7, 13); sometimes the battle is so hard that only his power gained through prayer is successful (9.14–29). Jesus' power and the violence of the conflict is also demonstrated in his control over the storms of nature (4.35–41; 6.46–52).

Although Mark calls Jesus 'Teacher', he gives little actual teaching. His Jesus is a powerful figure, working acts of dynamite, which bring him into conflict with his own family and town and with the religious leaders. He is indeed a beast of conflict, a lion roaming territory to establish his control over the real source of opposition, the devil himself, likened by Mark's traditional teacher, Peter, to a lion (1 Peter 5.8). Mark sets a lion to conquer a lion, and his Jesus is more powerful.

The lion and his pride   *The role of the disciples*

A lion must have his pride—and a rabbi, his disciples. However, are Jesus' disciples his 'pride and joy'? On the one hand, they are the people Jesus calls to share his roamings and his battles; on the other hand, their attention seems frequently to wander off, and Jesus has a constant battle to make them understand. So what are we to make of Mark's picture of Jesus' closest friends and followers?

The disciples are called 'immediately' and they obey and follow him (1.16–20), as does Levi (2.14). During the first half of the gospel, they witness all the relentless activity of Jesus, rushing around with him, listening to his teaching and sharing his conflicts. Jesus chooses 'those whom he wanted . . . to be with him', as his named apostles, to do all that he does—to preach and teach, exorcize and heal (3.13–15). At first, they do this with him; then, like any good teacher, he sends them out to practise on their own (6.7–13), followed by a 'report back' (6.30–31). Mark is keen on three-fold patterns in his narrative, and here we have the three classic steps of discipleship: to be called, to be chosen and to be sent out.

This is all positive. After the misunderstanding of Jesus' family and the conflict with the authorities, here are some people who respond positively to Jesus, relieving the gloom and opposition. As 4.11–12 makes clear, things are hidden to those outside, but the disciples are given the 'secret of the kingdom of God'—the *musterion*,'mystery'. Unfortunately, during the next few chapters, things become a bit of a mystery to the poor disciples. It begins with Jesus' question 'do you not understand?' (4.13)—and the frustration in his voice grows: 'they did not understand' (6.52); 'do you also fail to understand?' (7.18); 'do you still not perceive or understand? Are your hearts hardened? Do you have eyes, and fail to see? Do you have ears, and fail to hear?' (8. 17–18). Even after Peter's flash of divine inspiration recognizing Jesus as Messiah (8.29), he quickly slips back into misunderstanding Jesus' prediction of his Passion and has to be rebuked, 'Get behind me, Satan!' (8.33); elsewhere in Mark, it is demons and violent winds which are 'rebuked' by Jesus (1.25; 4.39; 9.25). A week later, at the transfiguration, Peter babbles inane suggestions out of terror (9.5–6), and when they come down the mountain, they find that the other disciples have failed to help the epileptic demoniac (9.18, 28). Meanwhile, James and John think the whole point of discipleship is to get the best seats in heaven—not realizing that Jesus' throne is to be a cross (10.35–45).

After the three-fold pattern of being called, chosen and sent out, now the disciples fail in threes as well. Their apparent lack of faith and understanding is repeatedly lamented by Jesus in the three boat scenes (4.40–41; 6.50–52; 8.14–21). They cannot comprehend the three Passion predictions, despite the increasing detail (8.32–33; 9.32; 10.32–41). Eventually, they fall asleep in Gethsemane three times (14.37, 40, 41) and are involved in three final actions—betrayal by Judas, denial by Peter and abandonment of Jesus by them all (14.43–6, 50, 66–72). No one can accuse Mark of not making the point clear! Once again, it is too clear for Matthew and Luke; as with their versions of Mark's account of Jesus' family, so here also they tone down the disciples' failure. Luke omits Peter's misunderstanding and Jesus' rebuke (Lk. 9.18–22), while Matthew changes the exorcist's 'rebuked' into the milder 'he said to Peter' (Matt. 16.23)! As for James and John asking for the seats of honour, Luke leaves it out completely, while Matthew has their *mother* make the request (Matt. 20.20–22). Matthew and Luke are not alone in suggesting that Mark has been harsh on the poor disciples. Some modern commentators suggest that the disciples get such a bad press in Mark that there must be a deliberate attack or polemic here against them; it is suggested that perhaps they represent some group of leaders opposed to Mark's community.

However, this does not explain all the positive material about the disciples being called, chosen and sent out, and having the secret of the kingdom revealed to them (4.11–12). Despite their increasing obtuseness, Jesus continues to explain 'everything in private to his disciples' (4.34); he gives them the little direct teaching Mark contains about clean food and unclean thoughts (7.17–23), the meaning of discipleship as self-denial (8.34–8; 9.30–50; 10.23–31, 35–45), the power of prayer (11.20–25), and the End-times (13). Despite his subsequent misunderstanding, it is still Peter who makes the Messianic confession (8.29); it is Peter, and James and John, despite their desire for self-advancement, whom Jesus invites to witness the transfiguration (9.2–8), and watch with him in the garden (14.33).

The fact is that, unlike the opponents of Jesus who are seeking to trap him, the disciples in Mark do want to understand and they do want to follow; it is as though it all gets too much too fast for them. If the lion has to roar at them for their slowness, it may also be because he is rushing on ahead to face the climax of his struggle. There is something in Mark's account which invites the reader's sympathy for their terror on the mountain (9.6) and their exhaustion in the garden: 'the spirit is willing but the flesh is weak' (14.38). Yes, they deserted him and fled—but he said they would (14.50 and 27). Yes, Peter denied him—after he had 'followed at a distance' when the others had fled (14.54); his rash love for Jesus prompted his promise to follow (14.29), and that same rashness led him into the high priest's courtyard where his nerve finally failed. Despite all the failures, the disciples' story is left open at the end of Mark. Unlike the other gospels, there is no resurrection appearance to bring them restoration—just Jesus' promise to 'go before you to Galilee' (14.28), confirmed by the man in white (16.7).

Thus, in its openness, the disciples' story becomes our story. Will they go to Galilee? Will we? If we are using biography as a key to understanding the gospels, it makes more sense to see the disciples' incomprehension in Mark as telling us more about his portrait of *Jesus* than about the disciples: he is someone whom people find hard to understand and tough to follow—so perhaps the audience can take comfort if they too sometimes find discipleship difficult. The lion roars and rushes on ahead. At the very end of the Narnia stories, Aslan leads them all in a headlong chase into his country: '"Come farther in! Come farther up!" he shouted over his shoulder. But who could keep up with him at that pace?' (C. S. Lewis, *The Last Battle*, Puffin/Penguin, 1964, p. 144). Mark's account suggests that disciples of every age struggle to follow the lion; but he promises to meet us in Galilee where he first called and chose us to be his pride—and joy?

What kind of animal is this creature?

Identity and interlude, Mark 8–10

So, everybody misunderstands Jesus during the first half of this gospel—his family (3.21–35), the crowds (4.10–12), the Gerasenes (5.17), his own home town (6.1–6), the religious leaders (7.6, 8.11–12) and even the poor disciples (8.17–18). However, this is hardly surprising: Jesus bounds on to the stage from nowhere and, once he has arrived, he does not make things very clear. The parables are such favourite stories to us today that the 'meanings' are clear; but to the first listeners, they would have seemed like riddles. Wandering teachers in the East, then and now, use riddles to force the hearer to think new thoughts in new ways—and Jesus was an expert riddler, that 'they may indeed listen, but not understand' (4.12). He was a master of irony—'Is it lawful to do good or to do harm on the sabbath, to save life or to kill?' (3.4)—and paradox—'Those who want to save their life will lose it, and those who lose their life for my sake, and for the sake of the gospel, will save it' (8.45). Thus, Mark's Jesus strikes amazement, fear, and awe into people (e.g. 1.22; 2.12; 5.15; 6.2; 7.37), an inscrutable and enigmatic figure. If the text is transparent to the reader, it is because Mark wants us to understand what he is saying; within his text, the evangelist portrays Jesus baffling opponents and disciples, family and crowds, alike.

So, who is he? He is announced as 'Jesus Christ, the Son of God' at the start and this is confirmed by the voice at his baptism (1.1, 11), but only we hear these comments. The wandering rabbi with his band of disciples was a familiar sight in first century Palestine. There is evidence in the text that many saw him as an apocalyptic or eschatological prophet, announcing the End like so many others of his day (6.14–16; 8.28). None the less, the question of his identity is repeatedly asked: who, or what have we here? (1.27; 4.41; 6.3). Jesus' Messianic identity has been known to us, the audience, since the outset; but when some in the story recognize him, this enigmatic character binds them to secrecy. Jesus silences the demons he confronts (e.g. 1.25, 34; 3.12) and the people he heals (1.44; 5.43; 7.36). Curiously, in Mark, it is the lion who puts muzzles on people! Yet, the more he tells them to be quiet, the more it is made known.

Mark raises further questions by the titles he uses for Jesus. Jesus is declared 'Son of God' by the author (if we accept this reading in 1.1), by the voice from heaven (1.11; 9.7), and by demons (3.11; 5.7)—but by no human being while he is still alive. Instead, despite his secrecy, Jesus is quite happy, openly in the presence of scribes, Pharisees, and disciples alike, to call himself the 'Son of Man' (2.10, 28; 8.31, 38; 9.12, 31; 10.33, 45; 13.26; 14.21, 41). Now much scholarly ink has been spilt over the meaning of this phrase recently—but let it suffice to say that in Jesus' own language, Aramaic, it was a roundabout way for people to refer to themselves, as in 'one has to earn one's keep, doesn't one?' So, this slightly curious, enigmatic turn of phrase fits Mark's portrayal of a riddling Jesus teasing his audience well—especially if they recall the equally enigmatic reference to 'someone like a son of man' coming on the clouds of heaven in Daniel 7.13.

The pivot of Mark's narrative comes in chapter 8. Up to this point, Jesus has been portrayed as a powerful healer-exorcist in conflict with practically everyone except his own disciples, and even they are confused. Now the veil is about to be lifted. First, we have a little 'hinge' paragraph in which a blind man is healed—but for once, not 'immediately': after the first touch from Jesus, he can see, but it is all rather blurred, men look like trees, and he needs a second dose (8.22–26). Significantly, Matthew and Luke both omit this story, probably because Jesus does not get it right first time. However, perhaps Mark is giving us an image of what is about to happen. Jesus asks his disciples about his identity. After various popular hypotheses are given, he presses the point: 'And you [in the plural], who do *you* say I am?', and Peter declares, 'You are the Christ' (8.29). The secret is out! The muzzle is off—but only for a moment, for he then 'sternly ordered' (the word is used for muzzling demons in 1.25 and 3.12) them to keep it quiet. Instead, he explains 'quite openly' with no secrecy, that his Messiahship will involve suffering, rejection and death. For Peter, however, it is like the blind man: a sudden flash of insight, and now this talk of suffering has blurred it all again. So he protests, and receives not so much a second touch, but more of a cuff around the ear from the lion as Jesus 'rebukes' him with the charge of being inspired by Satan (note the exorcist's word again, omitted by Luke and toned down by Matthew).

From here, Mark's structure leads to the Cross, with Jesus' three prophecies of his suffering and death (8.31–2, 9.31–2, 10.33–4) and his teaching about self-denying discipleship for the sake of the kingdom (8.34–38; 9.42–50; 10.23–31, 35–45). The lion is about to become a victim, yet the other side of his identity is not lost. Peter's confession is confirmed by witnessing the transfiguration and the voice declaring Jesus' divine Sonship (9.2–8); and when they return from the mountain-top experience to the harsh reality of the cosmic conflict, Jesus is still powerful enough to triumph where the disciples failed (9.14–29).

So what are we to make of this powerful Son of God/ Christ figure winning all his battles on the one hand, and the enigmatic, self-deprecating Son of Man *en route* to a painfully ignominious death? Has Mark become as confused as he makes the disciples out to be? One recent scholarly view has interpreted Mark's depiction of Jesus as a 'reverse aretalogy'. On this basis, Jesus is at first seen as a miracle-wonder-worker, according to the conventions of 'aretalogy', which is a kind of biography of a so-called 'divine man', *theios aner*. Mark is trying to show that this is a wrong understanding, providing a corrective Christology with his increasingly dark stress on suffering, leading to the Cross.

While it is true to say that Mark does have a strong theology of suffering, there are problems with this view. First, it is far from certain that there was a single concept of a divine man, or indeed of aretalogy itself, around at this time. Second, it is odd that God's own estimate of Jesus' identity as his Son given through the heavenly voice at his baptism and confirmed at the transfiguration (1.11; 9.7), is somehow 'wrong' or in need of correction. Instead of seeing a conflict between the Son of God Christology and the Son of Man Christology, it can be argued that the two are not correctives, but complements to each other, mixing the inward and the outward, the divine and the human, the vindication and the humiliation. Jesus never rejects Peter's acclamation of him as Christ; he just redefines what 'Christ' means—that he should suffer and die. The Cross has overshadowed everything since the start; now it is moving into the foreground. Right at the heart of the gospel, both Jesus' identity and destiny are made manifest—and for those who follow, the path of discipleship will be inevitably cruciform.

This is confirmed by the increasingly detailed prophecies through this middle movement of Mark's symphony (to use our earlier image), and by the way these chapters act as a bridge section geographically. While Jesus roams over the northern territories in the first eight chapters, this material happens on a southward journey. The lion of the north is heading to his lair. Caesarea Philippi, the site of Peter's confession (8.27) is in the extreme north, towards the source of the Jordan. Gradually, we have moved south 'on through Galilee' (9.30), and down into Judea (10.1) on the way to Jerusalem (10.32). On this very road Jesus gives his most explicit prediction of his Passion (10.33–34), and prophesies that the ambitious James and John can share his baptism by martyrdom; Christian greatness is seen in service, even as 'the Son of Man came not to be served, but to serve and give his life as a ransom for many' (10.35–45).

Finally, another 'hinge' passage occurs, like the one which began this section (8.22–26), concerning the healing of a blind man (10.46–52). Mark is making a point by this deliberate repetition, placing this incident carefully as Jesus sets out for the final stage from Jericho to walk up the road to Jerusalem (v.46). A blind beggar, Bartimaeus, hearing that it is 'Jesus of Nazareth', ignores the home town label and calls out a Messianic appeal, 'Jesus, Son of David, have mercy on me' (v.47). For the first time, Jesus does not respond with a command for secrecy; it is the crowd who tell Bartimaeus to be quiet (v.48). Jesus accepts both the acclamation and the beggar, granting his request. This time there is no blurring or second touch: the key word is back, 'and immediately (*euthus*) he regained his sight and followed him *en te hodo*' (v.52). This is another example of Mark's riddling: it could just mean 'along the road'—and for those still blind, this is the obvious translation. However, the gospel began with the call to 'prepare the way' (*hodos*) and make it 'straight' (*euthus*, 1.2–3). The sower sowed some seed 'along the way' (4.4, 15) lest the multitude faint 'on the way' (8.3); the disciples were questioned about his identity 'on the way' (8.27), and they disputed about greatness 'on the way' (9.33), 'the way' which leads to Jerusalem (10.32). Now the middle slow movement is over: Jesus' identity is no secret, the blind see, and follow Jesus 'on the way, straightaway' (10.52)—*euthus* and *hodos* are reunited, and the pace is hotting up. The lion is off again, heading for his lair, and the reader, with eyes open, had better keep up!

Jerusalem—the lion's lair or robbers' den?

The Temple, Mark 11–13

Mark's gospel is like a symphony in three movements: we rushed through the first half in a flurry of activity, power and conflict, healings and exorcisms (1–8.26); the second

movement was an interlude at a slower pace, giving time
to consider Jesus' identity, and moving geographically
towards Jerusalem. Now we enter the final movement, and
both time and space come into play. After his total lack of
interest in dates and times so far, Mark carefully orders this
final week, day by day:

Holy Week in Mark

Sunday	11.1–11	The entry into Jerusalem and the Temple; departure in the evening (v.11).
Monday	11.12–19	The fig tree *en route* to Jerusalem; incident in the Temple; departure in the evening (v.19).
Tuesday	11.20–13.37	The fig tree *en route* to Jerusalem again; discussions in and about the Temple.
Wednesday	14.1–11	Two days before the Passover; the anointing and Judas.
Thursday	14.12–72	One day before the Passover; the Last Supper and arrest.
Friday	15.1–47	The crucifixion and burial of Jesus.
Saturday		The sabbath rest (15.42, 16.1).
Sunday	16.1–8	What happened next.

After the vagueness earlier in Mark's gospel, this attention
to time and space is striking; the chronological focus even
details hour by hour on Friday (15.1, 25, 33, 34, 42), while
spatial awareness concentrates around the Temple (11.11,
11.15–16, 11.27, 12.35, 13.1, 13.3). While Jesus taught
daily in the Temple (14.49) there is a growing anti-Temple
theme, leading to the accusation that Jesus prophesied its
destruction (14.58). As well as these changes of time and
space, the content of this final section differs from the rest
of the gospel: the healings and exorcisms disappear, the
conflict gathers momentum and the teaching moves from
the kingdom and discipleship to questions of authority and

suffering. The lion comes to his lair—but finds it is a robbers' den; the king of beasts comes to his throne—but is rejected.

Jesus' entry into Jerusalem is another example of Mark's ironic riddling. The excuse for the disciples to take the colt—'The master needs it'—implies that the owner has sent them to fetch it; the crowd shout the welcome to pilgrims who come 'in the name of the Lord' to a festival in Jerusalem (Ps. 118.26); after Jesus has looked around like any pilgrim (or tourist), he leaves (11.11). Unlike Matthew and Luke, who make this entry the prelude to the 'cleansing' of the Temple, Mark has the two events on two separate days. It all seems rather low-key on the surface. However, the word for 'the master', *ho kurios* (v.3), also means 'the Lord' (v.9); a king has the right to commandeer transport, and, according to the Mishnah (*Mishnah, Tractate Sanhedrin*, 2.5), a king's horse should be ridden by no one else, as is true of this colt (v.2); and third, an extra cry is added to the usual pilgrim's welcome: 'blessed is the coming kingdom of our father David' (v.10). Jesus began his walk to Jerusalem with the accolade of the blind man 'Son of David'; now, finally, people 'prepare the way of the Lord' (1.3) with their cloaks and branches (11.7–8). For those prepared to look closer into Mark's riddle, the irony is made plain; the king comes to claim his kingdom—truly the act of a lion.

Another of Mark's 1-2-1 'sandwich' formations follows: on Monday morning on the way into Jerusalem, Jesus tries to find fruit on a fig tree, although it is not the season for figs—and, rather unreasonably, curses it for being barren (11.12–14); then he clears the money-changers and merchants out of the Temple, and goes home himself (11.15–19); third, the fig tree is discovered to have withered as they come to the Temple the next morning, which causes Jesus to teach about prayer (11.20–25). As before with the 1-2-1 connection of Jesus' family with the Beelzebul controversy, so here also Matthew and Luke do not share Mark's enthusiasm for sandwiches: Luke omits the fig tree altogether at this point (Lk. 19. 28–48), preferring to have a parable earlier about someone wanting to destroy a fig tree with no fruit

(Lk. 13.6–9), while Matthew places the whole incident the day *after* the Temple cleansing, so the tree withers immediately it is cursed (Matt. 21.18–19).

The sandwiching of these stories is thus Mark's way of making an illustration clear. The connection is obvious, and it explains Jesus' apparently unreasonable cursing of a fig tree for not producing fruit out of season. The fig tree is still common in Palestine and Syria, and the years it takes to grow and develop made it, and the vines which often grow with it, a natural symbol for prosperity and peace (see 1 Kings 4.25; Micah 4.4). Both plants were frequently used by the prophets as symbols for Israel's fruitfulness in loyal times (Hosea 9.10) and barrenness when unfaithful: 'When I wanted to gather them, says the Lord, there are no grapes on the vine, nor figs on the fig tree' (Jer. 8.13; see also, Hos. 9.16; Micah 7.1). So, in Mark's sandwich, the cursing of the fig tree is not pique from a hungry Jesus, but a dramatic illustration of the story in the middle: just as the fig tree is cursed for not bearing fruit, so the Temple is cursed for not being 'a house of prayer for all the nations' (11.17). Regardless of the season, the fig tree and the Temple, and all Israel, should have recognized the coming King—and burst into fruit. The other symbol comes in the parable of the tenants of the vineyard producing no fruit (12.1–12), while Jesus later uses the blooming fig tree to symbolize preparing for the master's unexpected coming, regardless of season (13.28–36).

So, Mark's narrative sandwich technique explains not just the 'bread' of the fig tree story, but also the 'filling'— the demonstration in the Temple (11.15–18). The precise nature and historical consequences of such an act are debated among scholars; it is unlikely that one person could have cleared the Temple courts without being cut down by the Jewish Temple police or the Roman garrison next door. However, the *symbolic* intention of Jesus' act is clarified, not just by the fig tree symbol, but also by his quotation of a similar protest by Jeremiah in the earlier Temple, prior to *its* destruction (Jer. 7.1–15). Jesus translates the symbol into direct teaching about the coming destruction of the Temple in the eschatological discourse (13.1–2). Finally, we note the extra layer around the fig tree and the Temple, giving a 'double-decker' sandwich: this section is preceded by the entry which raises the question of Jesus' identity and authority (11.1–11), and it is followed by controversy with the Jewish leaders, again about identity and authority (11.27–33). Thus, the whole of chapter 11 is a 0-1-2-1-0 formation, stressing the urgency of the coming crisis about Jesus' identity and authority to raise the themes for the next two chapters.

Mark 11

vv. 1–11	Entry—who is this?	0
vv. 12–14	Fig tree is cursed	1
vv. 15–19	Temple incident	2
vv. 20–25	Fig tree withered	1
vv. 27–33	Dispute—who is this?	0

In 2.1–3.6, Mark linked together 'controversy stories' between Jesus and various Jewish authorities, leading to the Pharisees and Herodians joining forces to plot against him (3.6). Now we have another string of controversy stories (11.27–12.44) as the same unlikely alliance tests Jesus (12.13), but now they are joined by the scribes, chief priests and elders (11.27, stirred into action by his Temple demonstration?), and the Sadducees (12.18). One common link is Jesus' authority, directly raised in 11.28, hinted at—perhaps sarcastically—in 12.14, and referred to by Jesus himself in 12.35–37. However, the theme of bearing fruit also runs from chapter 11 through these stories: like the fig tree and the Temple, the tenants in the vineyard also refuse to give their fruit to God (12.1–12). Jesus the Riddler's clever answer to the riddle about taxes neatly challenges his questioners to 'render to God the things that are God's' (12.13–17). One scribe does get things right, agreeing with Jesus that rendering the fruit of love to God and one's neighbour is more important than anything, including the Temple system of sacrifice (Mk. 12.32–34, omitted in Matthew and Luke's accounts, Matt. 22.34–40; Lk. 10.25–28). Finally, after a

brief attack by Jesus on the Jewish authorities (12.35–40, which is vastly expanded in Matthew and Luke), this theme comes to a climax with the story of the widow who, unlike all the others, *does* bear fruit and gives her all to God (12.41–44).

Not bearing fruit brought rejection and destruction for the fig tree and for the tenants. In chapter 13, Jesus leaves the Temple and sits down opposite on the Mount of Olives to prophesy the rejection and destruction not just of the barren Temple, but of Jerusalem and even the world. The spatial language of 'leaving' and 'opposing' the Temple (13.1, 3) cannot be accidental. Those who turn their back on a lion tend to be eaten!

Unlike the rest of the gospel, the so-called 'Markan Apocalypse' of chapter 13 is a continuous sequence of direct teaching, apparently delivered to a few disciples, but actually aimed at the early church suffering persecution and tribulation. This material, different from the rest of the gospel, was probably collected together at an early stage in the early church; however, Mark was still happy to include it in his gospel here. Its strong theme of suffering may have been appropriate for Mark's audience, especially if they had suffered in the persecutions of Nero at Rome, or were experiencing the horrors of the Jewish War of AD 66–70, leading to the destruction of the Temple.

Mark has obviously reworked it with his typical three-somes: there are the three calls to be aware and alert (13.5, 9, 23); three signs of the End (vv.14, 24, 28), and three calls to be awake (vv.34, 35, 37). References to the 'desolating sacrilege', and learning from the fig tree (13.12, 28) take us back to the sandwich in 11.12–24. The warnings that discipleship will involve suffering (13.9–11) pick up the teaching of the gospel's middle section about taking up the cross (8.34–38; 10.35–45), while the splitting of families (13.12–13) reminds us of Jesus' difficulties with his own family (3.20–35) and his response to Peter (10.28–31). Through it all, the theme of conflict is overriding, from wars and natural disasters (13.7–8) to trials, and the destruction of Jerusalem (13.9–11, 14–16), eventually reaching cosmic

proportions (13.24–25). The description of suffering 'for
my sake' (13.9, 13) and the warning not to confuse the false
Christs (13.21–22) with the unexpected arrival of the Son
of Man (13.26–36) suggest that the readers will continue
the same conflict which Jesus experienced throughout this
gospel. So, despite its apparent self-containment, this chapter
brings together all the main strands of the gospel so far.

The lion has come to his lair and has been rejected; now
he faces the final conflict—and we expect him to respond
with a roar and conquer. In fact, he is about to die; but this
chapter is placed here to assure us that, whatever sufferings
he or his followers must suffer, on the cosmic level there is
another story still being played out where he is king.

In at the kill   *The Passion, Mark 14–15*

At last we come to the ending—the Markan Passion, a dark
scene to which the whole gospel has been leading. Jesus has
made his way to Jerusalem, and this geographical concentration has brought the conflict into focus: a lion's story
should always end with a kill, but the narrative has warned
us that it is the lion who will die. Mark's gospel has been
often called a 'Passion narrative with a long introduction';
equally, the carefully linked sequence of the Passion was
thought to be the only narrative to have come to Mark from
his sources. However, attention to Mark's literary skill as an
author questions these assumptions. To see 80 per cent of a
work as mere introduction is rather an overstatement;
equally, however the Passion material came to Mark, the
same mind has carefully narrated it to form a fitting climax
to his story. The gospel is a life of Jesus—and ancient
biography usually gave detailed attention to the subject's
death as a way of summing up his life. To go back to the
image of our symphony, now all the themes—power and
conflict, discipleship and misunderstanding, identity and
authority, kingship and suffering—come together to build
the final climax.

The lion symbol brings clear images of kingship to us,
yet we have seen a tension between the exalted language of

Christ and Son of God (from the voice and from demons) and Jesus' preference for Son of Man and suffering language. The appearance of Jesus before the Sanhedrin brings it all together. In another Markan sandwich, Peter is 'warming himself at the fire' (14.54 and 67) either side of Jesus' interrogation (14.55–65). A contrast may be implied between the warmth of the fire for Peter and the coldness of the questions to Jesus—but there is an explicit disjunction between the denial by Peter (14.66–72), who had previously confessed Jesus, and affirmation by Jesus of an identity he had previously tried to keep secret. In 14.62 all three titles come together: the High Priest asks Jesus directly, 'Are you Christ' (picking up 1.1 and 8.29), 'the Son of the Blessed One?' (implying the title 'Son of God' used by the demons and the voice in 1.11 and 9.7; as only a human being, the High Priest still avoids the direct form). Jesus responds with a direct 'I am' (echoing the divine name of Exodus 3.14), but then returns to Son of Man, not for riddling humble self-affirmation, but for the glorious figure of Daniel 7.13. The High Priest's reaction of tearing his clothes emphasizes how stupendous a claim has been made.

The kingly language is full of typical Markan irony throughout this section. It begins with the cries of the crowd (11.10), and it continues with Jesus being anointed by a woman (14.3–9), usually a sign of the crowning of a king (1 Sam. 10.1; 16.13), but which Jesus interprets as anointing for burial (14.8). It comes like a regular refrain through chapter 15: Pilate asks Jesus if he is 'King of the Jews', and describes him as this to the crowd (15.9, 12); Jesus is mocked as king by soldiers (15.16–20) and by the scribes and priests (15.32); over his head the execution charge proclaims, 'The King of the Jews' (15.26). Mark makes full play of the irony that Jesus is mocked as king, yet that very mockery proclaims his true identity.

Kings are usually in control, and the lion has been actively rushing around—but now things are different. The Greek verb *paradidomi*, to 'hand over' to someone else, is used by Jesus of himself in the second and third Passion predictions (9.31; 10.33), and for the fate of his disciples in the three apocalyptic warnings (13.9, 11, 12). Now it is used about Jesus no less than ten times (14.10, 11, 18, 21, 41, 42, 44; 15.1, 10, 15). Thus, Jesus has become increasingly passive; others are in control now as they 'hand him on' from one to another—from Judas to the Jewish leaders to Pilate, and then to the soldiers to be crucified. Typically, Mark heightens the tension by opening up three opportunities for the lion to jump free: in Gethsemane (14.35–36), in Pilate's attempt to release him (15.9), and the mockers ironically pointing out his ability to save himself and come down from the cross (15.30). However, it is all to no avail; he is completely in their power now. Even the bystanders are aggressive, and he is reviled by everyone—the passersby, the chief priests and scribes, and *both* of those crucified with him (15.29–32). Ironically, this lack of control asserts the final sovereignty of God as Jesus' opponents actually fulfil his task through the very attempt to stop him by mockery and crucifixion. As the active lion is now passive, so too his roar is silenced and muzzled: Mark allows Jesus to speak only the requisite three times—to accept his identity from the High Priest and from Pilate (14.62; 15.2), and the final cry of desolation to God (15.34). The rest of the time, he stresses that Jesus was silent (14.61; 15.5). Once again, we are reminded of Aslan as the lion who suffers, whose mane is shaved and jaws are muzzled to be mocked as only a big pussy and who is then killed at the Stone Table (*The Lion, the Witch and the Wardrobe*, Puffin/ Penguin, 1959, pp.139–40).

The whole scene of the crucifixion itself is one of unrelieved darkness (both metaphorical and physical, 15.33), suffering, abandonment and desolation. Jesus has been gradually abandoned and rejected by everyone; the crowning desolation comes with the only word in Mark spoken from the cross: 'My God, my God, why have you forsaken me?', the opening words of Psalm 22. The mocking of Jesus (15.29, 31) also alludes to this Psalm, 'All who see me mock at me; they make mouths at me, they shake their heads' (Ps. 22. 6–7). In a recapitulation of the baptism, *schizo* reappears—but only the veil of the Temple is split this time; the heavens remain closed and the voice of 1.11 and 9.7 is silent now. The ultimate irony is that Jesus' words, as so often before, are again and finally misunderstood: 'Listen, he is calling for Elijah' (15.35). So they wait—but no one comes; even this last hope of rescue is dashed and Jesus dies alone, forsaken and rejected (15.37).

Here, then, the various threads are brought together: the bounding lion is tied up, the enigmatic prophet is still misunderstood, the disciples' little faith has deserted them, the conflict is lost, and the Son of Man dies as he prophesied. Yet at this moment, the first human being recognizes that he is the Son of God—but it is not a disciple, nor a religious leader, nor even one of his own people, but the Roman centurion (15.39). It is a typical biographical motif to sum up the subject's life with a one-line, epigrammatic epitaph; the secret which no one saw while he was alive is now manifest—but it is too late. All that remains is to give him burial in a stranger's tomb (15.40–47).

To most people in the ancient world, the attempt to see meaning in the death of a crucified criminal would have been pointless. Crucifixion was completely forbidden for Roman citizens, and only used for slaves and aliens; to anyone educated in the Greek philosophical tradition of divine detachment from the world, it would have been utter foolishness to seek theological profit from this death, while to a Jew anyone hanged on a tree was cursed (Deut. 21. 22–23; see also 1 Cor. 1.23). It is, therefore, Mark's sublime theological achievement to bring his narrative to a climax at the cross with such a dark picture. Here must be the answer to all the puzzles and riddles of this gospel. The enigmatic figure, so often misunderstood by family and disciples, and opposed by religious and political authorities, shows his power and identity in his final conflict by suffering the ultimate degradation and even abandonment by God himself. So, it must also be for Mark's audience; throughout the gospel, especially in the middle section on discipleship and in the apocalyptic warnings of 13, there have been hints that this is the fate of the church. Those who believe that following the way of the crucified one is a bed of roses have forgotten about thorns, says Mark. Yes, Jesus *is* the Son of God, powerful and mighty in his cosmic struggle, and that is not to be forgotten; but there was no last minute miraculous escape for him—and those who follow should expect no less.

'Rose like a lion'?   *The Resurrection, Mark 16.1–8*

When we come to Mark's account of the resurrection, we find things are no better: the early church Fathers can talk of Jesus rising triumphant like a lion—but that image cannot be based on Mk. 16.1–8. Like so much of his gospel, Mark's ending is full of enigma, fear, and awe. Instead of tying things up with a nice, happy ending, this story just leaves us with more questions. Where has Jesus gone? Why do the women, who witnessed the stone being put into place on Friday evening (15.46–47), only think about the difficulties of moving it away once they are actually on the way to the tomb (16.3)? Who, or what, is the young man in white (16.5)? After all Jesus' commands for secrecy and silence in this gospel, now, when the women are finally instructed to tell others, why do they keep it secret out of fear (16.7–8)? Thus, the gospel which has been full of secrecy and hiddenness concludes with an empty tomb and an absent Jesus.

The promise in 16.7, that the disciples will see Jesus in Galilee, picks up Jesus' own prophecy at the Last Supper of their desertion, and his promise to go before them to Galilee (14.27–8). Here one of Mark's main narrative lines terminates, but does not conclude. The sympathetic reader wants to know what happened to the poor disciples: does it all come right in a joyful reunion at the end? We will have to look to other evangelists for that. In keeping with Mark's picture of discipleship throughout the gospel, this question is left open; for Mark's story of Jesus becomes the story of his followers, and their story becomes the story of the readers. Whether they will follow or desert, believe or misunderstand, see him in Galilee or remain staring blindly into an empty tomb, depends upon us.

This all assumes, of course, that the gospel ends at 16.8. Certainly, it stops here: the two alternative endings of 8b and 9–20 are missing in the ancient manuscripts, are of a different style, and are based on the later gospels. They may have been composed to fill the 'gap' left when the original ending was lost—but perhaps there never was an 'ending'. In literary terms, the 'closure' of a narrative can draw the threads together, balance the beginning—or leave things deliberately open; it could be argued that 16.1–8 does all three of these. If Aslan is not a tame lion, Mark is not a comforting book. We have used the image of the lion for Jesus rather than the author—but perhaps there is something of the lion in Mark, too, always jumping around, but full of power and waiting to strike. In the *Book of Kells*, as well as the lion on the front page of Mark, there is a smaller lion crawling up the edge of the opening illuminated letter of the text itself in 1.1 (see Figure 4); in its mouth is a bearded human figure which it is apparently about to devour. Is the lion Jesus about to consume the evangelist Mark? Or is the lion the evangelist, getting his jaws around the helpless figure of the reader? We do not know, but perhaps the gospel should carry a health warning!

Whether the original stopped here, or around here, Mark's narrative as we have it now ends as abruptly as it began. There was no introduction or background to Jesus' arrival, and none for his departure. No one knew where he came from; no one knows where he has gone; and not many understood him when he was here—an enigmatic figure whose power was realized in suffering and whose kingship was proclaimed in death. To conclude with our central image of Mark's Christology, the lion bounds on, roars, and bounds off again, calling us to see him, in Galilee, somewhere.

> '"Then he isn't safe?" said Lucy.
> "Safe?" said Mr Beaver, "Who said anything about safe? 'Course he isn't safe. But he's good. He's the King, I tell you."'
>
> (*The Lion, the Witch and the Wardrobe*, Puffin/Penguin, 1959, p. 75)

Figure 4 Detail from the opening words of
St Mark's Gospel, *The Book of Kells*, Folio 130R.

3

The Teacher of Israel—
Matthew's Jesus

The human face   *Symbolism and meaning*

Our detailed consideration of Mark has demonstrated the
person-centred reading of the gospels as biographies. About
90 per cent of Mark (around 600 verses) is repeated in
Matthew, slightly abbreviated into some 523 verses to
comprise about roughly half of his gospel. Yet, despite this,
Matthew's overall picture of Jesus is rather different. He
gives us a much fuller portrait, conforming his gospel closer
to biography with his extra material in the birth and resurrection narratives, plus a lot more teaching.

If Mark's gospel is dark and riddling, Matthew has
'become like a child' (Matt. 18.3, rather than Mark's
'receive', Mk. 10.15): my five- and seven-year-old daughters
are constantly asking, 'Why? What for? I don't understand
—explain, Daddy, please'. If Mark's Jesus is enigmatic and
ambiguous, Matthew's view is much more explicit and
transparent; he makes clear the dark corners of Mark's
narrative. If Mark's account is concerned for the hiddenness
of God and the absence of Jesus, Matthew gives us the
revelation of God in the presence of Jesus (1.23; 28.20).

The symbol always associated with Matthew is the human
face. In the sculptures and religions of the ancient Near
East, animals represented divine powers and attributes, but
the human form symbolized revelation and intelligence.
According to the Old Testament, the definition of being
human is to have understanding (Prov. 30.2) which comes
through the Spirit of God in a person (Job 32.8); human beings,

Figure 5 St Matthew, *Lindisfarne Gospels*, Folio 25b.

male and female together, are made in the image of God
with dominion over the earth (Gen. 1.26–27; Ps. 8.5–8).
Understanding, and perhaps dominion too, suggests the
symbol of a teacher. Matthew includes most of Mark's busy
activity of Jesus to form half his gospel, the basic narrative.
A further quarter of the gospel, about 280 verses compris-
ing the teaching and sayings of Jesus, is shared with Luke,
material taken from Q perhaps. The remaining quarter
(called 'M' by scholars for short) is material which appears
only in Matthew. These verses reveal Matthew's particular
interests, and, in this, the most Jewish of gospels, Jesus is
not just the rabbi, but the human face of God, the revealer
who has dominion and authority as the Son of God. The
human face is less graphic as an image than Mark's lion,
but for Matthew the crucial question is simply this: how
does a good Jewish boy like Yeshua ben Joseph of Nazareth
set out to become the Teacher of Israel, yet end up founding
a Gentile church?

Where is he who is born King of the Jews?

Infancy narratives, Matthew 1–2

Mark begins with 'the beginning of the gospel of Jesus
Christ', but Matthew picks another key word—*genesis*: 'the
book of the generation (*biblos geneseos*) of Jesus Christ,
son of David, son of Abraham' (1.1). Immediately we have
a phrase used repeatedly in the book called 'Genesis', (see
Gen. 2.4; 5.1); no one could miss the allusion, implying a
recreation of the creation in the arrival of Jesus. Furthermore, while Mark's Jesus bounds on to the stage fully
grown, Matthew makes his account more like ancient
biographies by providing some information about Jesus'
ancestry, origin and birth. Ancient lives often included these
topics, before jumping ahead to the subject's arrival on the
public scene, although this was usually done briefly, rather
than the full treatment we expect in modern biography.

Matthew calls Jesus 'Christ' (as in Mark), but he changes
Mark's 'Son of God' into 'Son of David, son of Abraham'.
Immediately we are taken into the Jewish background of

the Teacher of Israel. While only blind Bartimaeus names Jesus 'Son of David' in Mark as he goes to Jerusalem, in Matthew he is called 'Son of David' much earlier, both by the crowds (12.23; 21.9, 15) and by people seeking his aid (9.27; 15.22; 20.30–1). 'Son of Abraham' is not mentioned in Mark at all; for Matthew this title looks back to the great hero of Genesis—but also forward to the fulfilment of God's promise to Abraham that *all* nations would be blessed through him (Gen. 12.3; 18.18; 22.18; 26.4). This will be fulfilled through the worship of foreign wise men (2.1–12), and the faith of a Roman centurion (8.10–11); Israel will learn that God can make children for Abraham from stones (3.9), and Jesus' final commission will send the disciples to the Gentiles (28.19).

These two themes—the Jewishness of David and Abraham and the intrusion of Gentiles—both appear in Matthew's version of the genealogy of Jesus. It is structured in three groups of fourteen names, from Abraham to David (1.2–6), David to the Exile (vv.6–11) and thence to Jesus himself (vv.12–16)—and Matthew makes the numerical point clear in his summary (v.17). Like Mark, Matthew likes the number three, while fourteen is the sum of the numerical value of the Hebrew letters in David's name. Jesus, says Matthew, is descended from Abraham and is 'Son of David' three times over!

Yet this Jewish genealogy includes four strange women —Tamar (v.3), Rahab and Ruth (v.5), and 'the wife of Uriah' (v.6). They all have Gentile connections: Tamar was probably a Canaanite (1 Chron. 2.3–4); Rahab was a native of Jericho before the conquest (Joshua 2.1); Ruth was a Moabite (Ruth 1.4); and Uriah was a Hittite (2 Sam. 11.3). They also bring sexual irregularities into the scheme: Tamar pretended to be a prostitute to conceive Perez and Zerah from her dead husband's father (Gen. 38.7–9, 13–30); Rahab was a prostitute (Josh. 2.1; 6.22–25); Ruth was left childless by her husband's death, and contributed to the genealogy by his kinsman, Boaz (Ruth 1.5; 4.13); the mention of Bathsheba only via her husband's name reminds us of David's adultery and murder (2 Sam. 11–12). The conception of Jesus by Mary, the wife of Joseph (1.16), is the supreme irregularity—yet it is all in God's plan (1.17): Jesus is the one through whom the promise to Abraham for all nations will be fulfilled, and who will be accused of being a friend of Gentiles and sinners.

After the genealogy, 1.18 repeats the key word again: 'the *genesis* of Jesus Christ was like this', and we are off into Matthew's so-called 'birth narrative'—except that there is no narrative of the birth. Instead, Matthew recounts Mary's pregnancy from Joseph's viewpoint (1.18–25), followed by the visit of Gentile wise men to the infant at some indeterminate point after the birth (2.1–18). The hints of sexual irregularity from the genealogy are picked up, with Joseph's desire to spare Mary disgrace (1.19); instead of his planned quiet dismissal, the intervention of an angel causes Joseph to accept the shame himself by taking Mary as his wife and receiving the child into his genealogy (1.25). None the less, both the narrator (1.18) and the angel (1.20) stress Jesus' divine Sonship, conceived by the Holy Spirit—and the absence of marital relations between Joseph and Mary underlines the point (1.25). The sequence from a basic description to an appearance of an angel and a prophecy about the child, all stressing God's involvement, would remind Matthew's readers of similar birth stories in the Old Testament (e.g. Sarai, Abram and Hagar in Gen. 16 or the birth of Samson in Judges 13).

When our children were born, like many proud parents we agonized for a long time about choosing names, consulting various lists of names and their meanings. Names were important in ancient biography, too, as a clue to the future identity or activity of the subject. Matthew follows this convention with the angel's explanation: 'Jesus' is the Greek form of 'Joshua' (or *Yeshua*), meaning 'God is salvation' (1.21). The name 'Jesus' occurs in Matthew about 150 times (almost as often as in Mark and Luke combined), yet he is never addressed by name here (unlike Mk. 1.24; 5.7; 10.47, omitted in Matt. 8.29; 20.30), and only rarely do others refer to him by name (21.11; 26.69, 71; 27.17, 22, 37). Matthew keeps this name with its declaration that 'God is salvation' for himself as narrator when telling his story about Jesus. Jesus is also Emmanuel, meaning 'God with us': this gospel is about the presence of God, not his enigmatic hiddenness—and this verse forms a neat 'book-end', propping up this end of the gospel, balanced by the very last promise to be with us always in 28.20. So, these personal names in chapter 1 make it very clear exactly who Jesus is.

In chapter 2, various geographical names tell us where Jesus has come from. After the prophecy of his birth in chapter 1, Jesus has already been born at the start of chapter 2—in Bethlehem, apparently where the family live already. Then wise men from the East come to Jerusalem with another name: 'where is he who is born King of the Jews' (2.2). Geography moves with the wise men to Bethlehem (v.8) and their return by a different route (v.12); the flight of the holy family into Egypt (v.14); the massacre of the infants in Bethlehem (vv.16–18), and the return from Egypt to settle in Nazareth (vv.19–23). Unlike Mark, Matthew is quite clear who this Teacher of Israel is, and where he has come from and been.

Although the story is told from Joseph's perspective, as he receives dreams and warnings, yet the constant stress on 'the child and his mother' (2.11, 13, 14, 20) reminds us that Jesus is the Son of God; Joseph is never told 'take *your* child'. Jesus' divine identity is revealed by being worshipped (2.2, 8, 11). While this word is rare in Mark and Luke, not only is Jesus worshipped in Matthew as a baby, but this continues throughout his life by those who come to him—lepers, women, disciples (8.2; 9.18; 14.33; 15.25; 20.20; 28.9, 17).

Thus, these opening chapters make clear Jesus' Jewish origins and divine identity—but they also hint of rejection: the unholy alliance of Herod and the chief priests and scribes, the dreams and the warnings, and the massacre of the innocent, all foreshadow the later conflict in this gospel between Israel and her Teacher. The Old Testament atmosphere continues with the fulfilment of various prophecies (1.22–3; 2.6, 15, 17, 23). Not only do we have fulfilment, but there is also recapitulation of Moses' story: the infant is saved from an evil king intent on slaughtering babies (Exodus 1.15–2.10, cp. Matt. 2.16–18); he has to flee for his life and grow up in another land (Exod. 2.15–22, cp. Matt. 2.13–14) to return only after the death of the King (Exod. 2.23, cp. Matt. 2.19–20), which also involves taking wife and sons (Exod. 4.20, cp. Matt. 2.21). So, Matthew suggests that Jesus is not only Son of David and Son of Abraham, but he is also another Moses, the Liberator, to teach Israel again that 'God is salvation'.

Thus, these opening chapters proclaim Jesus' identity clearly from the title, the genealogy and the 'birth' stories; there is no 'Markan secret' in this gospel. In addition, Matthew cleverly weaves many of his themes into these beginnings: God is active in salvation for his people Israel through this new Abraham–Moses–David figure—yet he hints that Israel may reject him, while the Gentiles, who are involved irregularly in Jesus' ancestry and worshipfully at his birth, may receive the fulfilment of God's promise to Abraham of blessing for all nations.

Another Moses?   *Beginning ministry, Matthew 3–8.1*

Old Testament allusions in the next section develop further the picture of Jesus as the Teacher of Israel, another Moses. Chapters 3–8.1 move around the river Jordan, the wilderness, and the mountain—all immediately reminding us of the stories in Exodus. Israel in Egypt was described by God to Pharaoh as 'my firstborn son' (Exod. 4.22); they went across the waters of the Red Sea (Exod. 14.21–22), and were tested by God in the wilderness for forty years (Deut. 8.2); Moses went up on to the mountain to receive the teaching of God (Exod. 19.20), and afterwards came down to the people (Exod. 19.24–25); at the end of the testing in the wilderness, Moses was taken by God to the top of a mountain to survey the country he could not enter (Deut. 3.27; 34.1–4); after his death, the Israelites crossed the river Jordan led by Joshua, whose name means 'God is salvation' (Josh. 3).

Now we have another prophet in the wilderness (Matt. 3.1–3); Jesus, 'God is salvation', comes to the river Jordan (3.13), and is declared by God to be 'my Son' (3.17); like Israel, he is then led into the wilderness to be tested for forty days and nights (4.1–2), at the end of which, he too is taken to a high mountain to be shown the kingdoms of the world (4.8); he also goes up on to a mountain to give his teaching to Israel (5.1), and afterwards comes down to the people (8.1). In this way, Matthew carefully and cleverly draws his portrait of Jesus as another Moses, the new Teacher of Israel—but with one further geographical point. While Moses is only shown the land of Israel from his mountain (Deut. 34.1–4), Jesus sees 'all the kingdoms of the world' (Matt. 4.8); furthermore, only Matthew points out that Jesus went to live in Capernaum, in 'Galilee of the Gentiles', so that those in darkness might see light (4.13–16). As in the infancy stories, so here we see hints that the Gentiles will be blessed by this Teacher of Israel.

Comparison with the other gospels brings out the subtle differences in Matthew 3–4. While Matthew and Luke share most of John the Baptist's preaching (compare Matt. 3.7–10, 12 with Lk. 3.7–9, 17), only Matthew says that it was directed at the Pharisees and Sadducees (3.7), as Jesus' criticisms will also be later (Matt. 23). Only Matthew tells us that John hesitated about baptizing Jesus (3.14). Some early Christians found it hard to understand why Jesus was baptized: for example, in the *Gospel according to the Hebrews*, Mary suggests being baptized to Jesus, who replies that he has no need to go since he is sinless (preserved in Jerome, *Against Pelagius*, III.2). Matthew does not go that far, but Jesus' reply introduces two of Matthew's favourite words, 'to fulfil all righteousness' (3.15). Finally, while in Mark Jesus sees the heavens torn apart and hears 'you are my Son' (Mk. 1.10–11), in Matthew the heavens are publicly opened and the voice announces to everyone, 'This is my beloved Son'. Again, there is no secret about Jesus' identity here: he is the Son of God, endowed with the Spirit (Matt. 3.16–17).

Jesus' identity is also the key to the temptation story

(4.1–11). The first two temptations recall the voice from the baptism, challenging Jesus as Son of God to produce food or test God's promises by defying gravity by jumping from the temple pinnacle. Once again, we remember Israel's experience in the exodus: the humbling by hunger was met with manna (Deut. 8.3), while Israel tested God at Massah (Deut. 6.16). Jesus' responses also come from this section of Deuteronomy: 'one does not live by bread alone' (4.4, quoting Deut. 8.3b) and 'do not test the Lord your God' (4.7; Deut. 6.16). Finally, as Moses surveyed Israel from Pisgah (Deut. 3.27; 34.1–4), so, from a high mountain, Jesus is shown all the kingdoms of the world, but refuses to claim them by worshipping the devil (4.10, quoting Deut. 6.13). Jesus will receive all authority not from the devil, but from God; instead of worshipping the devil, he will be worshipped when he sends his disciples on a mission to all the kingdoms from another mountain, in another of Matthew's 'bookends' (28.16–20). Thus, in the wilderness, Jesus triumphs where Israel failed, and he goes to live in 'Galilee of the Gentiles' (4.13–15), where, like Moses, he will teach Israel from the mountain (5.1; 8.1). This opening section introduces three themes: mountains, fulfilment of scripture, and the identity of Jesus.

Mountains

For some strange reason, human beings connect mountains with God. In many ancient religions, worship took place on the 'high places'. Even today, we talk of 'mountain-top experiences', despite having left behind the notion that mountains are closer to God's supposed dwelling in the sky—although high-altitude jet travel does make some people pray more fervently! Mountains were also important in Israel's religious development, especially Sinai (and its connection with Moses) and Zion (forever linked with David). On these two mountains, God met his people in covenants. At Sinai (also known as Horeb) the law and covenant were given (Exodus 19–24; 1 Kings 8.9), and Elijah renewed his vision of God (1 Kings 19.8). Zion was

David's city (2 Sam. 5.6–10; 6.1–19), the site of worship in the Temple (1 Kings 6; 2 Chron. 3–5; see especially Psalms 120–134) and the future venue for the final consummation, both for Israel (Is. 35.10; Jer. 31.12; Ezek. 20.40, and chapters 40–48) and for all the nations (Micah 4.1–2; Zech. 14.2, 16–17).

Thus, for Israel, mountains represent revelation, the presence of God, worship and consummation, all of which appear in Matthew's mountain-top presentation of his Teacher. Some of the mountains are taken from Mark: Jesus went to the mountain to pray (Matt. 14.23, = Mk. 6.46); he is transfigured on a mountain (Matt. 17.1, = Mk. 9.2); he enters Jerusalem over the Mount of Olives (Matt. 21.1, = Mk. 11.1), where he also delivers the apocalyptic discourse (Matt. 24.3, = Mk. 13.3), and goes to pray in Gethsemane (Matt. 26.30, = Mk. 14.26)—but Mark does not develop the settings. For the apocalyptic discourse, Luke omits the Mount of Olives and concentrates on the Temple (compare Lk. 21.5–7 with Mk. 13.1–3); Matthew omits the Temple and stresses the Mount for the eschatological consummation (24.3). Matthew also introduces new mountains: the final resistance to Satan takes place on a 'very high mountain' (4.8); Jesus goes 'up on the mountain' to teach his new law and covenant (5.1); he also goes 'up on the mountain' for healing (15.29–31), and feeding of the four thousand (15.32–39); on a final mountain in Galilee, the risen Christ receives worship and commissions his disciples (28.16–20).

In this subtle way, Matthew uses mountains to point to Jesus' identity: he is another Moses who teaches and miraculously feeds multitudes on mountains; he is the Son of David, prophesying the eschatological consummation from Zion; he is the Son of God, worshipped by all the nations on the mountain. He is the Teacher of Israel—and more: he is the presence of God, not in a cloud hovering over a mountain, but in a person among his people.

Fulfilment of the law and the prophets

Second, this new Teacher of Israel fulfils scripture repeatedly during the opening chapters, and Jesus uses scripture to defeat Satan in the wilderness. Matthew has about sixty references or quotations from the Old Testament—three times as many as Mark. Ten passages are introduced by the phrase 'this was to fulfil what had been spoken through the prophet' (the virgin birth, 1.22–3; the flight to Egypt, 2.15; the massacre of infants, 2.17–18; Nazareth, 2.23; living in Galilee, 4.14–16; healing and ministry, 8.17; 12.17–21; parables, 13.35; the entry to Jerusalem, 21.4–5; and Judas' 'blood money', 27.9–10). Other passages also refer to the fulfilment of scripture (2.5–6; 13.14–15; 26.54, 56).

The Teacher of Israel fulfils Israel's scripture—but also the law. Only in Matthew has Jesus come not to abolish the law and the prophets, but to fulfil them (5.17–20). This passage steers a middle course between two tendencies which were prevalent at the time: Matthew resists 'antinomian' opposition to the law, but he argues against the law-centred approach of Rabbinic Judaism. Equally, Matthew depicts Jesus interpreting the commandments regarding murder, adultery, divorce, swearing, retaliation and the love of enemies: 'You have heard that it was said . . . but I say to you . . .' (5.21–48). In a non-legalistic way, he goes beyond the letter of the law to the interior meaning, but without any antinomian weakening of the law. Twice in Jesus' response to criticism from Pharisees, Matthew inserts Hos. 6.6, 'I desire mercy, not sacrifice' (9.13, cp. Mk. 2.17; and 12.7, cp. Mk. 2.25–27). The Teacher of Israel uses love to interpret the law. Similarly, Matthew omits Jesus' approval of the lawyer who asked about the greatest commandment (Mk. 12.34; Lk. 10.28); to love God and one's neighbour is central, but Matthew alone continues, 'on these two commandments depend all the law and the prophets' (Matt. 22.36–40). Luke has the simple 'Golden Rule' to do to others as we would be done by (Lk. 6.31), but Matthew adds 'for this is the law and the prophets' (Matt. 7.12). Thus, through this fulfilment of scripture and the law,

Matthew stresses the continuity of Jesus the Teacher with Israel's scriptures and traditions.

The identity of Jesus

As well as showing how Jesus fulfils the law and prophets, Matthew also comments that 'something greater than the temple is here' (Matt. 12.6). Jesus' identity runs through the opening chapters as the fulfilment of the Jewish hopes—a new Abraham to bless the Gentiles, a new Moses to enter all the lands, a new David to bring the consummation, even a new Israel to triumph in the wilderness. While Jesus refers to himself as 'the teacher' in 26.18 (and the 'one teacher' of 23.8), the disciples never call him teacher in Matthew: only opponents and questioners use this address (8.19; 9.11; 12.38; 17.24; 19.16; 22.16, 24, 36)—and 'Rabbi' is the salutation from the traitor, Judas (26.25, 49). Jesus is the Teacher—but he is much more than this: in Matthew, the disciples and those who ask for help call him *kyrie*, 'Lord' (8.2, 6, 8, 21, 25; 9.28; 14.28, 30; 15.22, 25, 27; 16.22; 17.4, 15; 18.21; 20.30, 31, 33; 26.22).

Matthew's account of Peter's confession goes beyond Mark's 'You are the Christ' to add 'the Son of the living God' (Matt. 16.16, cp. Mk. 8.29). Here Jesus' Messiahship is not secret: his divine Sonship was clear throughout the infancy stories (2.15), and was declared publicly by the heavenly voice (3.17). Satan questions this in the temptation, but Jesus does not need to prove it (4.1–11). He is worshipped as the Son of God by the disciples in the boat (14.33), recognized by Peter (16.16), and this is repeated by Caiaphas (26.63). Yet, Jesus answers with 'Son of Man' to both Peter and Caiaphas; the divine and the human fit together as the Son of Man will come in power (10.23; 13.41; 19.28; 24.30). The titles all converge in Matthew's unique parable of the judgement of the sheep and goats, where the Son of Man is also a King and Lord, dependent on his Father (25.31–46).

Jesus' divine origin is also shown by the worship given to the infant (2.2, 11), by the synagogue ruler (9.18), and by the disciples in the boat (14.33) and after the resurrection (28.9, 17). Furthermore, Matthew has a tendency to remove Mark's references to Jesus' human feelings: pity for a leper (Mk. 1.41: Matt. 8.3); anger at the Pharisees (Mk. 3.5: Matt. 12.13); Jesus' amazement and inability to do miracles in Nazareth (Mk. 6.6: Matt. 13.58); Jesus' exasperation with Pharisees (Mk. 8.12: Matt. 16.2), indignation with disciples (Mk. 10.14: Matt.19.14), and love for the young ruler (Mk. 10.21: Matt.19.21). He omits Jesus' questions which might imply his lack of knowledge (see Mk. 5.9, 30; 6.38; 9.12, 16, 21, 33; 10.3; 14.14). These subtle changes produce a different atmosphere, reminding us constantly that, as well as the human face of God, Jesus is also nothing less than the Son of God.

Thus, Matthew has handled Jesus' identity cleverly through these opening chapters. While Jesus as Teacher of Israel repeats Israel's history through his own experiences —as an infant, in Egypt, in the wilderness, on mountains, and at the river Jordan—it is insufficient for Matthew to see Jesus as just a new Moses or a new David. He is all that the great heroes were—and more. He fulfils Israel's history and scriptures, law and prophets. He is *the* Teacher, the son of Abraham, the Davidic Messiah-King, the Lord, the Son of God himself, present with his people. So, what will he have to say, and how will he be received?

The new teaching   *The Discourses, Matthew 5–7, 10,*
13, 18, 23–5

While Mark has very little actual teaching, Matthew builds the character of Jesus as the Teacher of Israel, and structures the gospel around his five great blocks of teaching— the discourses punctuating the narrative (5–7, 10, 13, 18, 23–25). Detailed comparison with Mark and Luke reveals how carefully Matthew has worked on these chapters. Some parts of Matthew's sermons have come from Mark: chapter 10 has verses from Mk. 6.7–13; chapter 13 includes parables from Mk. 4.3–34; chapter 18 has teaching from Mk. 9.35–48 and 24 is similar to Mk. 13.5–37. Some of

Matthew's extra material is shared with Luke and probably came from Q: for example, some of the teaching in Matthew's continuous Sermon on the Mount (Matt. 5–7) is scattered in bits and pieces throughout Luke's gospel (Lk. 6.20–49; 7.1; 8.16; 11.2–4, 9–13, 33, 34–35; 12.22–31, 33–34, 58–59; 13.24, 25–27; 14.34–35; 16.13, 17, 18). Matthew takes these separate teachings from Q, completely re-orders and mixes them with his own special material to form beautifully crafted sermons as a complete, clear and concise exposition of the teaching of Jesus the Teacher.

All five sermons end with the same formula: 'and it happened when Jesus had completed these sayings' (7.28; 11.1; 13.53; 19.1; 26.1). The phrase 'and it happened' is Greek for the Hebrew *wayehi*, common throughout the Old Testament and traditionally translated as 'and it came to pass'. Matthew uses it to close each section of teaching to bring an Old Testament atmosphere to the words of the Teacher of Israel. His artistry and deliberate organization of his gospel is also seen in the way the five sermons balance each other in length and content:

```
5—7    ┌─ 107 verses teaching for the present ─┐
10     │ ┌─ 38 verses the church's mission ─┐  │
13     │ │  50 verses parables of the kingdom │ │
18     │ └─ 33 verses the church's life ─────┘ │
24—25  └─  94 verses teaching for the future ──┘
```

This makes chapter 13 structurally and theologically central —the parables end with the acceptance or rejection of Jesus the Teacher (13.51–58). This gives us a double-decker sandwich structure 1-2-3-2-1 for the nourishment offered by the Teacher in Matthew.

As Jesus teaches from mountains, the five discourses remind us of the five books of the Pentateuch; are these a new law from a new Moses? Since many other ancient works, including the Psalms, were organized into five books, perhaps this point should not be overdone. However, Matthew deliberately structures his gospel around these five sermons, moving from narrative to discourse, from the

Teacher's activity to his teaching, and back again, as he tells the story of Jesus. Furthermore, two levels appear: first, each discourse begins with Jesus speaking to his own audience, the disciples (5.1; 10.1, 5; 13.10–17; 18.1; 23.1; 24.3). Second, frequently he seems also to speak past them to Matthew's church: much of the instruction is for situations after Jesus' death and resurrection, and the constant address 'when you (plural) do . . .' or 'you shall . . .' challenges us, the hearers and readers. Jesus the Teacher is still teaching, says Matthew, even to 'the end of the age' (28.16–20). Such structural analyses call attention to the flow and development of Matthew's story of the conflict growing between the Teacher and Israel through the comparison and repetitions, balances and inclusions in his narrative. In our next section, we shall see how these sermons fit into the story line. First, however, we need to outline the content of the five discourses and their main themes.

Discourse 1—The Sermon on the Mount, 5–7

Matthew structures Jesus' teaching about the ethics of the kingdom of heaven in threes. It begins with nine Beatitudes—'Blessed are . . .'—in three groups of three (5.3–12). After calling the disciples salt and light (5.13–16), six (6 = 3 x 2) so-called 'antitheses' contrast the law—'it was said . . .'—with Jesus' demands—'but I say to you . . .' (5.17–48). Then, the three-fold practice of almsgiving, prayer (including the Lord's Prayer), and fasting is contrasted with that of the Jewish leaders (6.1–18). A three-part sandwich follows: trusting in riches or in God (6.19–33), judging others (7.1–6) and trusting God again (7.7–12). Finally, three warnings conclude: the two ways of the narrow gate and the wide road (7.13–14); false prophets and deception (7.15–23); and the two builders—the wise one on the rock, and the foolish on the sand (7.24–27). Through it all, Matthew stresses the theme of righteousness to God and our neighbour in all areas of life.

Discourse 2—The Mission of the Church, 10

Chapter 10 begins with the call of the disciples (10.1–4), while the sermon contains their instructions. They are to go only to 'the lost sheep of the house of Israel' (vv.5–6) preaching and healing (vv.7–15); they will encounter opposition and persecution, as Jesus himself has been treated (vv.16–25). The central section contains three encouragements not to be afraid (vv.26, 28, 31), followed by further warnings of persecution and division, rejection and acceptance (vv.32–42). Through this sermon, Matthew draws parallels between Jesus' task and the disciples' tasks—and so the missionary instructions pass on to the church down through time.

Discourse 3—The Parables of the Kingdom, 13

Here, Matthew collects parables depicting the progress of the kingdom—the sower (vv.1–9, 18–23), the weeds (vv.24–30, 36–43), the mustard seed (vv.31–32), leaven (v.33), hidden treasure and the pearl (vv.44–46), the net (vv.47–50) and the householder (vv.51–52). They all show the slow, and often secret, growth of the kingdom from small beginnings—and that its secrets are revealed to disciples, but hidden from those who do not understand (vv.10–17, 34–35).

Discourse 4—The Life of the Church, 18

This balances chapter 10's mission instructions with practical details. The church is to be characterized by humility, becoming 'like children' (vv.1–5) and not causing others to stumble (vv.6–9), following the pattern of God's own love, which is like a shepherd for a lost sheep (vv. 10–14); there are instructions about discipline (vv.15–20), but correction is to be given in an attitude of mercy and forgiving others 'seventy times seven' (vv.21–22), ending with the parable of the unmerciful servant, unique to Matthew (vv.23–35).

Discourse 5—Woes and the End, 23/24–25

Chapter 23 contains a sequence of woes against the Jewish leaders, scribes, and Pharisees, to which we shall return later. The final sermon of chapters 24–25 declares woe to the world, and the consummation of the kingdom. Chapter 24 follows Mark's eschatological discourse (Mk. 13) with its warnings of wars, persecutions, and the coming of the Son of Man. Matthew concludes with another triad, three parables about the judgement: the first, the wise and foolish maidens (25.1–13) and the third, the sheep and goats (25.31–46) are unique to Matthew, while that of the talents (25.14–30) has some similarities to Luke's parable of the pounds (Lk. 19.12–27).

Again, we shall follow Matthew's Semitic tradition by picking up three themes from the discourses: righteousness, the kingdom of heaven, and the church.

Righteousness, morality and judgement

Matthew's Teacher is concerned about moral teaching; one of his key words (occurring seven times in Matthew, once in Luke, and never in Mark) is *dikaiosyne*, justice or righteousness, with its adjective *dikaios* (fifteen times in Matthew; once in Mark; ten times in Luke). Joseph is *dikaios*, a righteous man (1.19). Fulfilling 'all righteousness' is why Jesus is baptized (3.15). It is something to hunger and thirst for (5.6), and to be sought (6.33); 'right' behaviour is required (5.10, 20; 6.1; 21.32). While Luke blesses the hungry (Lk. 6.21), Matthew has those who are hungry for 'righteousness' (5.6); while Luke tells us to 'seek his kingdom' (Lk. 6.31), Matthew adds 'and his righteousness' (6.33). Our 'righteousness' must not be paraded before others (6.1), but it must 'exceed that of the Pharisees' (5.20). Each sermon ends with judgement and reward: the reward of the wise builder, and the judgement of the foolish (7.24–27); the reward of the 'righteous' (*dikaios*) in welcoming the disciples (10.40–42); weeds/wheat and good/bad fish (13.36–50); removing the wicked from the

'righteous' (13.49); the judgement of the unforgiving servant (18.21–35); and the sheep, the 'righteous' (25.37, 46),
and the goats (25.31–46).

Salvation and mercy are gifts from God, shown by the
Master forgiving his servant (18.21–35), or in the mercy
to the blind (9.27–31; 20.29–34). Only Matthew has the
parable of the labourers in the vineyard, who all receive the
same reward regardless of how many hours they worked,
stressing the grace of God (20.1–16). Matthew's attitude to
righteousness reflects his approach to the law: it makes
stringent demands, but the essential element is the love of
God and neighbour (7.12; 22.34–40), 'mercy, not sacrifice'
(9.12; 12.7). Jesus came to call sinners, not the 'righteous',
dikaioi (9.12). Matthew's gospel stresses the love of God as
Father: while Mark calls God 'Father' occasionally (Mk.
8.38; 11.25–6; 13.32; 14.36), Matthew has it over fifty
times, mostly on the lips of Jesus in these discourses. Good
works are so that others may 'give glory to your Father'
(5.16); they should be done not for public reward, but in
secret to 'your Father who sees in secret' (6.1–4, 16–18).
Prayer is to the Father (6.6, 9), who will provide 'good
things' to his children (6.32–33; 7.11). God's fatherly
concern is also noted in the mission discourse (10.29–32)
and the church discourse (18.14). In the parables, the
'righteous' will shine in the kingdom of the Father (13.43).
Only God is to be called Father (23.9) and his kingdom is
prepared for the righteous at the judgement (25.34).

The kingdom of heaven

Matthew has the phrase 'kingdom of God' a few times
(12.28; 19.24; 21.31, 43), but normally he prefers 'kingdom
of heaven' (which occurs over thirty times) as a respectful
Semitic idiom to avoid mentioning God. The Greek word
basileia (for the Hebrew *malkuth*) is better translated as
sovereignty or kingship, rather than a specific 'kingdom'; it
is everywhere God's authority is acknowledged. Jesus is
called 'king' by the wise men (2.2), and in another of
Matthew's 'bookends', this is the charge on which he was

crucified (27.37). The kingdom was proclaimed as 'near at hand' both by John the Baptist (only in Matthew, 3.2) and by Jesus (4.17), and Jesus instructs his disciples to preach the same (10.7). It is a mixture of present reality and future hope: it 'has come upon you' in Jesus' exorcisms (12.28), yet it is still to come, to be prayed for and sought (6.10, 33). The central sermon is a collection of parables of the kingdom showing its growth (13.3–9, 18–23, 31–33), the mixture of good and bad up to the judgement (13.24–30, 47–50), and its great cost (13.44–45). The Son of Man will come in power to rule the kingdom of his Father (13.37–43; 25. 31–46). Matthew's version of the parable of the tenants in the vineyard (21.33–46) shows that Israel had the kingdom, but rejected God's servants, in two groups corresponding with the major and minor prophets (21.36); only Matthew concludes by warning that now she is losing it, and it will be 'given to a people that produces the fruits' (21.43). Thus, the kingdom is not the same as Israel, nor indeed the church—but the church is to call everyone to the kingdom for the eschatological consummation.

The church and the disciples

This leads us into the third theme of this gospel's teaching. Matthew is the only gospel to use the word *ecclesia*, church (three times, inevitably: 16.18 and twice in 18.17). Furthermore, the second and fourth discourses more clearly envisage a community with a mission (chapter 10) and discipline (chapter 18) than is found in the other gospels. Matthew depicts the Teacher of Israel summoning Israel to repentance, and calling a new body of faithful people when he is met with rejection.

The first disciples are called by the lake side (4.18–22, repeating Mk. 1.16–20); the calling involves leaving everything at Jesus' command, as Peter reminds him (19.27). While Lk. 9.57–60 does not identify the two potential followers, Matthew says that the first is a scribe, the second a disciple (8.19, 21). The scribe calls Jesus 'Teacher' (as only opponents do in this gospel), and offers to follow, rather than being called—and he is informed that 'the Son of Man has nowhere to lay his head' (8.19–20); the disciple calls him 'Lord' and is told 'Follow me' (8.21–22).

Matthew follows this with the stilling of the storm (8.23–27), the classic example of Matthew's editorial revision, or *redaction*. In Mark's account, 'they' take Jesus into the boat (Mk. 4.36); in Matthew, Jesus takes the initiative to get into the boat—and 'the disciples *followed* him' (8.23). 'Disciples' and 'following' give the moral of the story. When the storm comes, the disciples in Mark protest about Jesus' apparent lack of concern—'Teacher, do you not care if we perish?' (Mk. 4.38); in Matthew, their cry becomes a prayer—'Save ['Jesus' means 'God is salvation'], Lord [faith in their divine master], we are perishing'. So, Mark's hypothetical 'if' becomes real for the disciples in Matthew, and, by implication, for the readers when they are storm-tossed. Matthew transposes Mark's order: Jesus *first* questions their faith, *then* calms the storm (8.26) while Mark has it the other way around (Mk. 4.39–40). Further, while in Mark they have 'no faith' (Mk. 4.40), here Jesus calls them 'men of little faith' (8.26). This phrase, which does not occur in Mark, is used in Matthew when the disciples get anxious (6.30), or frightened (14.30–31), when they misunderstand him (16.8) or are unable to cast out the epileptic demon (17.20).

Such sympathy for the disciples and their 'little faith' creates a more positive picture than in Mark. Of course, they still betray Jesus (Judas, 26.25, 47–50), deny him (Peter, 26.69–75) and forsake him (26.31, 56)—and some still doubt even after the resurrection (28.17). However, unlike Mark's account, they do understand Jesus' teaching (13.51; 16.12; 17.13; cp. Mk. 6.52; 8.21; 9.32), and they believe and worship him (14.33). The word 'disciples' means 'learners', studying under one Teacher and master (10.24–25; 23.8–10) to become teachers themselves for Israel (10.5–6) and all the nations (28.20). The key is to obey Jesus' teaching like the wise man who built his house on the rock (7.21–27), and to respond to his invitation, 'Take my yoke upon you, and learn from me' (only found in Matthew, 11.25–7); eventually they do 'as Jesus directed them' (21.6; 26.19; 28.16). The disciples receive the teaching of the Teacher of Israel in his great discourses. They are the church, the new community of God's people, built upon the rock of Peter with the keys of the kingdom of heaven (16.18–19), and the authority to bind and loose given to them all (18.18). The Teacher has taught them—and they are to teach the whole world (28.20).

Conflict between the Teacher and Israel   *Matthew 8–23*

The intrusion of substantial non-narrative material in these sermons inhibits the movement of the plot. This mixture of Jesus' ministry and his teaching produces a more measured air; instead of the breathless dash of Mark's bounding lion, Matthew's human face of God pauses to catch his breath and to impart his teaching. Yet, there is still development of narrative flow as the stories of Jesus, the disciples, and the Jewish leaders all move inexorably towards a climax at the Passion. Furthermore, the discourses relate to the intervening material, and the sections of ministry prepare for the discourses. Let us look at each section in turn to see how the conflict grows and the plots thicken.

The development of the story

Jesus calls disciples in chapters 3–4, and gives them his teaching in the Sermon on the Mount, 5–8. Then, chapters 8–9 describe three triplets of miracle stories. The first three concern those who are marginalized—a leper, a centurion's servant, and a woman, Peter's mother-in-law (8.1–17). After two vignettes on discipleship (8.18–22), three stories depict Jesus' power over nature, evil and sin—the stilling of the storm, the exorcism of the Gadarene Legion, and the healing forgiveness for the paralytic (8.23–9.8). A second interlude on discipleship describes the call of Matthew and the controversy this aroused (9.9–17), before the final group of three miracles shows Jesus triumphing over death, blindness, and dumbness (9.18–34). As in Mark, the miracles are called 'mighty acts of power', *dunamis* (e.g., Matt. 11.20, 21, 23; 13.54; 14.2); signs are requested by Jesus' opponents (12.38–39; 16.1, 4) and signs and wonders are again the mark of false prophets (24.24). None the less, the miracles attract attention to Jesus and elicit the comment unique to Matthew, 'Never has anything like this been seen in Israel' (9.33). Unfortunately, the Pharisees reply that it is done through the prince of demons (9.34).

However, the Teacher of Israel still tries to get his message through. He gives his ministry of teaching, healing and exorcism to the disciples in the mission discourse of chapter 10. Only Matthew tells us that the disciples are sent, not to the Gentiles or Samaritans, but to the 'lost sheep of the house of Israel' (10.5–6). This discourse has its own storyline within its teaching: the mission is to Israel (10.5–6), but the disciples will be rejected and persecuted (10.17–25), yet there will be blessing for those who do help (10.40–42).

The next section of the Teacher's ministry depicts this rejection and conflict. Even John the Baptist misunderstands the nature of Jesus' Messiahship (11.2–19); 'this generation' does not want to respond (11.16–19), and its towns ignore Jesus (11.20–24). This causes Jesus to reflect on hiddenness and revelation (11.25–30), followed by conflict with the Pharisees over plucking grain and healing on the sabbath (12.1–14). Then, Matthew uses Isaiah's Servant Song to suggest that the Teacher will bring justice and hope to the Gentiles, if Israel rejects him (12.15–21, cp. Is. 42.1–4). Further conflict ensues in the Beelzebul controversy and the desire for signs (12.22–45). Finally, conflict with Jesus' own family is hinted at, but toned down from Mark's version (12.46–50, cp. Mk. 3.20–21, 31–35). After all this misunderstanding and conflict, it is not surprising that the central discourse of chapter 13 hides things in parables with a theme of judgement and warnings about being hard of heart (13.13–15).

From 14.1 onwards, Matthew's order of events follows Mark closely (Mk. 6.14ff). He begins by noting the death of John the Baptist, prefiguring the conflict awaiting Jesus (14.1–12). This is followed by the feeding of the five thousand

(14.13–21), and Jesus walking on water. Matthew follows
Mark closely for the first half, but then has the unique story
of Peter also attempting it; again Matthew gives us a prayer,
'Lord, save me', as Peter sinks, and Jesus calls him 'man
of little faith' (14.30–31, cp. the stilling of the storm in
8.25–26). Instead of the disciples' amazement and misunderstanding (as in Mk. 6.51–52), they worship Jesus and
declare their faith: 'Truly, you are the Son of God' (Matt.
14.33). Further opposition emerges from the Pharisees in
15.1–20, contrasted with Jesus' encounter with the Syro-
phoenician woman: only in Matthew's account does Jesus
declare that he was 'sent only to the lost sheep of the house
of Israel' (15.24); like the disciples, the woman kneels in
worship and prays to Jesus, 'Lord, help me' (15.25), and
declares her faith in him, 'O Lord, Son of David' (15.22,
27). While the disciples have 'little faith', Jesus responds,
'Woman, great is your faith!', and she receives her daughter's healing (15.28). Matthew is carefully suggesting that
as Israel questions and rejects her Teacher, so the Gentiles
begin to receive his benefits.

None the less, the 'God of Israel' is glorified by further
healings (15.29–31), and the feeding of four thousand
(15.32–9). Jesus' identity has been questioned during pre-
ceding chapters (8.27; 11.2–3; 12.22–23; 14.1–2), and the
Pharisees still seek signs (16.1–4)—but now at least the
disciples do understand (16.5–12, unlike Mk. 8.21). At
Caesarea Philippi, we only need a quick recap of the wrong
answers (16.13–14) and the right one given by Peter: 'you
are the Christ, the Son of the living God' (16.16). The
Teacher now begins to build a new community, with Peter
as the foundation—the first use of *ecclesia*, church; neither
the gates of Jerusalem, nor hell itself shall withstand it
(16.18). As in Mark, we have three Passion predictions
(16.21; 17.22–23; 20.17–19), teaching about discipleship
(16.24–28), followed by the transfiguration and healing of
the epileptic demoniac (17.1–21). Only Matthew gives us
the extraordinary story of Jesus paying his and Peter's
Temple tax out of a fish's mouth (17.24–27). If Peter was
fishing for favouritism, the Teacher stresses humility,

becoming like children (18.1–5), and instructs his followers for life together in the church discourse (occurring twice); Peter's authority to bind and loose is now given to them all (18.17–18), since reconciliation and forgiveness are to be the hallmarks (18.10–35).

After the church discourse, the journey to Jerusalem (chapters 19–20) and the clash with the Jewish leaders (chapters 21–23) again follows Mark fairly closely. The controversy with the Pharisees about marriage repeats Mk. 10.1–12, except for the famous 'Matthean exception' for divorce after *porneia*, sexual immorality, plus additional material about eunuchs, or sexual celibates (19.1–12). Jesus blesses the children (19.13–15), challenges the rich young man, and promises rewards for those who follow him (19.16–30). Matthew's unique parable of the labourers in the vineyard warns against expecting greater rewards than others (20.1–6). After the third Passion Prediction (20.17–19), the request from James and John is delivered through their mother according to Matthew (20.20–28, cp. v.20 with Mk. 10.35). Mark's blind Bartimaeus becomes two anonymous blind men outside Jericho (20.29–34).

For the entry into Jerusalem, Matthew's interest in fulfilment leads him to the image of the lowly king with colt and ass in Zech. 9.9–10. Unlike Mark's account, Jesus goes straight into the 'cleansing' of the Temple, which causes immediate controversy with the chief priests and scribes (21.10–17). Therefore, the fig tree has to be cursed the next day, and it withers immediately (21.18–22). The chief priests and elders dispute Jesus' authority (21.23–27), leading to three parables of judgement: the two sons, only in Matthew (21.28–32); the tenants in the vineyard with Matthew's unique warning in v.43 that the kingdom will be taken away from Israel and given to Gentiles (21.33–46); and the marriage feast (22.1–14), which is not in Mark and occurs much earlier in Luke (Lk. 14.16–24). Matthew's version is fuller, including the king destroying and burning their city (22.7), which may refer to the destruction of Jerusalem in AD 70; there is also the unique rejection of the person who is unprepared and not clad in the right garment

(21.11–14). This is a typical Matthean collection of three stories, and they are all applicable to the controversy with the Jewish leaders and the future inclusion of the Gentiles.

The whole range of Jewish leaders now conflict with this new Teacher (chief priests and elders, 21.23; Pharisees and Herodians 22.15–16; Sadducees 22.23; a lawyer 22.35). As in Mark, we have four controversy stories: tribute to Caesar (22.15–22); the resurrection (22.23–33); the Great Commandment, with the lawyer not praised, and Matthew's addition of the law and prophets (22.34–40); and Jesus' question about David's son (22.41–46). The Jewish leaders are reduced to silence, and they withdraw from the conflict (22.46), just as Satan did in 4.11. The stage is clear for Matthew's final discourse: according to this Teacher of Israel, her other teachers are hypocrites, even preventing others from entering the kingdom (23). This strong stuff leads into the apocalypse: chapter 24 begins by following Mark but its second half deals with the delay of the Coming and the need for continued vigilance (24.37–51); this material is scattered throughout Luke (Lk. 17.26–27, 30, 34–35; 12.29–40, 42–46) which implies that Matthew has taken it from Q and organized it here. The three parables of the Last Judgement, already discussed above, conclude chapter 25. When the Teacher has finished 'all these things' (26.1), the stage is now set for the climax of the Passion and the resolution of the various plot lines.

The development of the conflict

This analysis of the development of Matthew's narrative reveals the basic plot of a conflict between the Teacher of Israel and her leaders. The central character is Jesus, as the fulfilment of all Israel's hopes, who sets out on a mission only to Israel—to proclaim the kingdom of heaven. The paradoxical subplot in this most Jewish gospel is that the Jewish leaders become increasingly resistant to his teaching and the gospel responds with growing hostility, culminating in the diatribe of chapter 23. Meanwhile, the other subplot depicts the calling of disciples increasingly to understanding and faith in this Teacher—a new community which will also include the Gentiles. These three storylines will converge at the cross, where Jesus apparently fails in his mission to Israel and the disciples fail him, while the Jewish leaders appear to triumph; however, the Passion predictions in this section warn us of the ironical twist, that, in the will of God, the cross is the success whereby the Teacher of Israel will open the kingdom even to the Gentiles.

First, however, we must consider this portrayal of Israel, especially the Pharisees, in Matthew's gospel. How are we to understand the vitriol in his pen? In Matthean triadic fashion, three things are clear. First, his portrayal of Jesus as the Teacher of Israel, fulfilling the scriptures and recapitulating her heroes, suggests that the author and his intended audience are steeped in Judaism. Second, his attitude towards the Jewish leaders and Jerusalem does not seem calculated to woo them over, so it is unlikely that this gospel is designed for evangelism among the Jews themselves. Third, the depiction of the conflict and the language used suggests a lot of pain, bitterness, and anger. What kind of situation can fit these three conclusions?

Jesus was a Jew and all his first disciples were Jews. After his death and resurrection, the first Christians continued to see themselves as Jews, preaching the good news about Jesus among their own people. First century Judaism was a mixed culture with different groups, such as Pharisees, Sadducees, Essenes, Zealots, existing together; the early Christians seemed like just another group within Judaism. However, in the cosmopolitan cities of the eastern Roman empire, like Antioch in Syria, non-Jews began to want to join the church. Paul's letters reveal his deliberate mission to the Gentiles and the controversy this caused.

The Jewish Revolt of AD 66–70, culminating in the destruction of Jerusalem and the Temple, brought things to a head. The Romans no longer tolerated the Jews in Jerusalem, scattering them around the nations. Many of the different religious, cultural, and political groups within pre-war Judaism simply disappeared. In an attempt to provide cohesion and a renewed identity, some rabbis gathered at

Yavneh in the mid-80s; with the focus of Jerusalem and the Temple gone, they centred Jewish faith and worship around the law and the synagogue, giving rise to the Rabbinic tradition which has kept Judaism alive all around the world for two millennia. However, they also saw the growing Christian communities with their success among the Gentiles, as a threat, so the *birkath ha-minim*, the 'Blessing against the heretics' was included in the synagogue liturgy. This was a prayer for the destruction of the Roman empire and cursing heretics (*minim*) and *nosrim*, the 'Nazarenes', or Christians. From now on, Jewish-Christians could no longer worship with other Jews without cursing themselves, and the parting of the ways between the synagogue and the church took place around the end of the first century.

So, Matthew's portrayal of Jesus as Teacher of Israel reflects the bitterness and pain of this separation: it was not a polite agreement to differ, or an amicable settlement. Only Matthew warns that Christians will be delivered to councils, flogged in synagogues, and dragged before Gentile rulers, even by their own family (10.17–25). This also explains why, despite the Jewishness of the gospel, it is not aimed at Jews themselves: it is too late for the Jewish mission now. Instead, there is the theological problem for Jewish Christians of why Israel rejected her Teacher, the fulfilment of her scriptures and her hopes; of why the kingdom has gone to the Gentiles, and why Jerusalem was destroyed. If Matthew was written somewhere like Antioch during this separation in the mid-80s, his unique material and particular emphases make sense as answering these questions for hurting Jewish-Christians. He is like a scribe, bringing 'out of his treasure what is new and what is old' (13.52)—and holding them together. The synagogue is now 'their synagogue' (4.23; 9.35; 10.17; 12.9; 13.54) or 'your synagogue' (23.34), opposed to 'my church' (16.18). The parable of the marriage feast even contains a warning from Jesus that 'their city' will be burned (22.7), while the diatribe against the Pharisees concludes with a lament for Jerusalem, 'the city that kills the prophets and stones those who are sent to it!' (23.37–39).

The development of the story describes the rejection of the Teacher by Israel and the inclusion of the Gentiles. Jesus is Son of Abraham, through whom all nations will be blessed, with Gentiles in his genealogy (1.1–17). Although Jesus is 'sent only to the lost sheep of the house of Israel' (15.24) and sends his disciples similarly (10.5–6), Matthew's version of the tenants of the vineyard, the classic symbol of Israel in the prophets, concludes with the warning, unique to Matthew, that the kingdom will be taken away from them and given to 'another people' producing fruit (21.43). Significantly, Matthew never calls the church the new Israel (as Paul suggests in Gal. 6.16). He is well aware that the church is a mixture of 'the bad and good' invited to the marriage feast (22.10), of wheat and weeds (13.24–43) and of good and bad fish in the dragnet (13.47–50), all to be judged at the final consummation (13.30, 36–43, 49; 24.45– 25.46). In the intervening time, they are an egalitarian community who 'have one Teacher' (23.8–12) who gave them discipline and order (18.1–35) and sent them to teach all nations (28.19–20). As the Teacher was rejected by Israel, so too are his disciples.

The Teacher's suffering   *The Passion, Matthew 26–27*

Matthew includes nearly every verse of Mark's Passion in the same order, except little details about the young man (Mk. 14.51–2), and Simon of Cyrene's sons (Mk. 15.21b). Only about 26 verses are unique to Matthew (26.1–2, 25, 52–4; 27.3–10, 19, 24–5, 29, 51b–3, 62–66, all discussed below). Despite this similarity, Matthew's Passion is very different in its atmosphere. As throughout his gospel, his account is more awesome—and there is no ambiguity. Mark's Passion narrative depicted the suffering of Jesus as the final absence of God; here it is the means of his presence, underlining the identity of Jesus. As with Mark, the Passion narrative pulls the main themes of Matthew's gospel together: the history of Israel and God's salvation, the fulfilment of scripture, the portrayal of Jesus as the obedient Son of God, and the final conflict with the Jewish leaders causing the transfer of the kingdom to the Gentiles. The Teacher has given his teaching; now we have his example of righteous suffering.

While Mark portrayed Jesus as increasingly passive with control passing to others, Matthew shows that the Teacher of Israel goes to his death as a result of his own choice. Only Matthew gives us a fourth prediction of Jesus' Passion after 'all his sayings' to make the point: Jesus knows exactly what is about to happen (26.1–2). When he sends disciples into the city to prepare a room for the Passover, Jesus announces that his 'time' is at hand—*kairos* in Greek, the critical moment, rather than *chronos*, chronological time (Matt. 26.18, cp. Mk. 14.14). At the Last Supper, only Matthew has Jesus identify Judas as the betrayer in response to Judas' address, 'Rabbi', which is never used by other disciples in Matthew (26.25). When Judas again calls him 'Rabbi' in the garden, Jesus replies with 'Friend', asking why he has come, as though giving permission for his arrest (26.50). Only in Matthew does Jesus say that he has the power to call up 'more than twelve legions of angels' if he wishes (26.53). In fact, Jesus refused the temptation of angelic help in the wilderness (4.6–7), and he will do so again. Instead, he tells his followers to put away the sword —and so the Teacher follows his own teaching of non-violence (5.39–40). The reason is 'that the scriptures must be fulfilled'—back to Matthew's common motif throughout the gospel, that Jesus fulfils all of Israel's scripture and hopes, past and future.

Matthew alone in the gospels describes Judas' death (Matt. 27.3–10; Acts 1.18–20 has a different version). Only Matthew says that Judas actually asked for money—thirty pieces of silver (Matt. 26.15), the compensation value of a slave's life (Exod. 21.32) and also the redundancy pay-off for the rejected shepherd-prophet in Zech. 11.12. God tells Zechariah to throw the money into the temple treasury (Zech. 11.13); Judas throws it into the temple—and the priests buy a potter's field, alluding to Jeremiah's purchase of a field for silver (Jer. 32.6–15), putting the deed in a pot (Jer. 32.14), and reminiscent of his earlier visit to the potter's house (Jer. 18.2–3). So, this Old Testament background suggests that Jesus is the shepherd and prophet rejected by his people. Matthew inserts the story of Judas into Mark's flow to stress the guilt of the religious leaders, 'the sons of Israel' (27.9).

In another of Matthew's 'bookends', Pilate, a Western Gentile, calls Jesus 'King of the Jews' (27.11, see also vv.29, 37), as Gentiles from the East also sought 'the one born King of the Jews' in Jerusalem so long before (2.2). Only Matthew includes the dream of Pilate's wife (27.19) as the wise men, too, were warned in a dream of the murderous intent of another Jewish leader (2.12). She calls Jesus 'righteous'—Matthew's key-word, *dikaios*—as Pilate does in some manuscript versions of 27.24. The Gentile governor's hand-washing, unique to Matthew, again points out that Israel is responsible for her Teacher's death, as the people declare, 'his blood be on us and our children!' (27. 24–25). Jesus warned that the 'righteous blood of the righteous' would come upon them (23.34–36); now his words, and the prophets', are being fulfilled. This is the decisive moment, foretold uniquely in Matthew's version of the tenants of the vineyard (21.43) when Israel finally rejects her Teacher and the kingdom passes from them to another people. The ironic mocking of Jesus as king by kneeling soldiers in fact proclaims the truth; as at his birth Gentiles knelt to worship the king (2.2, 11), and in his ministry (15.25), so now they do so finally at his death (27.29).

The crucifixion scene is dark, as in Mark, yet supernatural. Matthew includes Jesus' name in the inscription (27.37, cp. Mk. 15.26). Both Jesus' human identity and his divine Sonship are made clear, as the taunts recall the Satanic temptation, 'if you are the Son of God' (27.40, cp. 4.3, 6); 'he trusts in God; let God deliver him now, if he wants to; for he said, "I am the Son of God"' (27.46) alludes to Ps 22.8, while Jesus quotes its opening desolation, 'My God, my God, why have you forsaken me?' (27.46). Matthew uses the proper Hebrew 'Eli' for Mark's Aramaic 'Eloi'; the hearers' misunderstanding about Elijah includes Matthew's crucial word, 'will save him' (27.49).

While the cry of abandonment goes unheard in Mark, here, Jesus' despair is answered by supernatural apocalyptic happenings: the splitting of rocks in an earthquake (*seismos*) is a sign of a theophany, the appearance of God (27.51; see Jdgs 5.4; 2 Sam. 22.8; 1 Kings 19.11; Pss. 68.8; 77.15–20) or the Day of the Lord (Haggai 2.6–9, 20–23). This gospel is no stranger to seismic disturbances; Jesus stilled the *seismos* on the Sea of Galilee (Matt. 8.24 cp. Mark's 'storm', Mk. 4.37) and he 'shook' Jerusalem at his entry (*eseisthe*, Matt. 21.20). The rising of the dead out of the tombs (27.52–3) reminds us of Ezekiel's vision of the Valley of Dry Bones (Ezek. 37.12–13).

Thus, while Mark's Passion becomes the climax of Jesus' suffering, in Matthew it is the climax of his Christology: Jesus' identity as Son of God is challenged by the leaders of Israel, but made manifest to all by the signs of the eschatological crisis. While only the centurion recognized Jesus in Mk. 15.39, here, everyone sees what happens and they are filled with awe, confessing Jesus as 'truly Son of God' (27.54). Finally, at Jesus' burial, Matthew does not mention that Joseph of Arimathea was 'a respected member of the Sanhedrin' (as in Mk. 15.43), since those leaders of Israel have rejected Jesus; instead, he calls him a disciple, one of the new community of faith brought into being by the Teacher's death (27.57).

The Teacher's vindication   *The Resurrection, Matthew 28*

This atmosphere of supernatural intervention openly visible to all continues into Matthew's resurrection account, as does his desire to tie up the loose ends and explain the difficulties. While Mark ends with a characteristically enigmatic empty tomb, a strange young man, frightened women who say nothing, and no appearance of Jesus, Matthew again has a supernatural earthquake witnessed openly by soldiers (28. 2–4), women who run off to tell others (28.8) and who see Jesus (28.9–10), the explanation about the tomb and the guards (28.11–15), and a final mountain scene (28.16–20). It is a carefully crafted chapter, with the typical three scenes arranged to balance believers (vv.1–10), opponents (vv.11–15), and believers (vv.16–20). The gospel which began with angels, mountains, and Gentiles coming to Israel, now ends with angels and a mountain where the new Israel is sent to the Gentiles.

Matthew likes to clarify Mark's hiddenness: the voice at Jesus' baptism was addressed not to Jesus alone, but to everyone, and the supernatural consequences of the crucifixion revealed his identity not just to a centurion, but to all present. So now, while in Mark the stone has already been moved (Mk. 16.3–4), here, both the women and the guards witness another earthquake and an angel (rather than Mark's enigmatic 'young man') descending from heaven to roll back the stone (28.2–4). However, Matthew does not go as far as the apocryphal *Gospel of Peter*, where the guards and priests witness huge angelic figures bring Jesus and a cross out of the tomb; here the resurrection appears to have already happened (according to the angel, 28.6). As the disciples in Matthew have some faith and understanding, similarly the women at the tomb have not only Mark's fear, but also joy and obedience; they run to tell the disciples, and are rewarded with an appearance of the risen Christ himself, whom they worship (27.8–10).

Now we have the final separation of the old Israel and the new community. Only Matthew notes what happened to Judas and the chief priests, and he continues to tie up loose ends with his unique account of the guard (27.62–66), and their bribing (28.11–15). This recalls the story of Judas, the only other place money occurs in Matthew. If Matthew composed his gospel for Jewish–Christians around the split with the synagogue, then this section makes good sense. The story of the theft of the body by the disciples is told 'among the Jews to this day' (28.15): apart from calling Jesus 'King of the Jews' (2.2; 27.11, 29, 37), this is Matthew's only use of 'the Jews'—and clearly they are now a different community from that of the evangelist, or the Teacher.

Meanwhile, the true Israel has gone to Galilee to meet its Teacher, once again on a mountain (28.16–20). Here, finally, we reach the climax of the gospel, and all the various themes come together. Despite their 'little faith' and their desertion at the Passion, the disciples finally go as 'Jesus directed them' (28.16). The identity of Jesus is clear, and they worship him on the mountain—although Matthew recognizes the mixed nature of the church by noting that even now some still doubted (28.17). The mountain reminds us of all the other mountains of this gospel, and all that Sinai and Zion meant for Israel; but this mountain is in Galilee—described by Matthew at the very start of Jesus' ministry as 'Galilee of the Gentiles' (4.15). Despite his stress on the mission to Israel, Matthew has been preparing us for this since the beginning, with Abraham and Gentiles in Joseph's ancestry, and the wise men from the East (chapters 1–2). Now that Israel has rejected her Teacher, the disciples receive the so-called 'Great Commission' to go and make disciples of all nations. They are now to become teachers themselves, teaching others what the Teacher commanded them (28.20). In the final 'bookend', reminding us of the initial mention of Emmanuel, 'God with us' (1.23), the Teacher promises to be with them for ever, 'even to the end of the age' (28.20). There has been no hiddenness nor absence of God in this gospel—and there is no ascension or departure of Jesus at the end. This is not an ending, but more of a beginning—and one which is all embracing: 'all authority' is given to Jesus, the disciples are to go to 'all nations', teaching them 'all things', and Jesus will be with them for 'all time'—for, according to Matthew's portrait, he is nothing less than the human face of God.

Figure 6 St Luke, *Lindisfarne Gospels*, Folio 137b.

4

The Bearer of Burdens—
Luke's Jesus

The powerful ox   *Symbolism and meaning*

After the human face of God in Matthew's Teacher of Israel
and the bounding lion of Mark, the next symbol for Jesus
might seem odd: to us, the ox seems somewhat slow and
stupid—and, indeed, some commentators have been known
to call Luke, with his long-drawn-out two volumes (the
Gospel and Acts), a bit of a 'plodder'! However, in biblical
times things were different. In the absence of machinery,
the ox was the ancient world's most powerful engine, a
symbol of divine strength in ancient representations from
Assyria to Egypt. Even the Pentateuch likens God to
'the horns of a wild ox' (Num. 23.22; 24.8). The common
description of the Lord as *'abir*, 'the Mighty One' of Jacob
or of Israel (e.g. Gen. 49.24; Ps. 132.2, 5; Isa. 1.24; 49.26;
60.16), has a verbal pun on *'abbir*, the mighty ox. Human
kings, like Pharaoh, could be likened to an ox, and the final
blessing of Moses on the Twelve Tribes calls Joseph 'a
firstborn bull . . . the horns of a wild ox' (Deut. 33.17).

The ox was the universal beast of burden—pulling carts
(Num. 7.3), carrying heavy loads (1 Chron. 12.40), ploughing (Deut. 22.10; 1 Kings 19.19), treading grain (Deut. 25.4;
Hos. 10.11)—the ox did it all. Proverbs is bluntly realistic:
'Where there are no oxen, there is no grain; abundant crops
come by the strength of the ox' (Prov. 14.4). The ox was
thus a symbol of wealth, important enough to be included in
the Tenth Commandment, 'You shall not covet your neighbour's . . . ox' (Exod. 20.17). The Israelites also knew that

99

such a powerful animal could be dangerous—hence the Mosaic laws about goring and compensation (e.g. Exod. 21. 28–32)! The ox was nothing less than king of the domestic animals. However, as well as the literal bearer of burdens, the ox was also used by the ancient Israelites to bear the burden of sin as a sacrificial animal (Lev. 4.3-21; Ps. 69.31). Oxen were sacrificed by David on the threshing floor of Araunah to avert the plague (2 Sam. 24.18–25), while Solomon sacrificed 22,000 to dedicate the Temple (1 Kings 8.63) which must have kept them busy; the priests had enough difficulty with the 600 sacrificed by Hezekiah (2 Chron. 29.33)!

So, while we use the modern plodding image a little, we also need to bear in mind all these ancient ideas of power and strength, work and wealth, sacrifice and the Temple; for Luke's portrait of Jesus is supremely the bearer of burdens, caring for all those who are burdened or suffering, and ultimately giving himself willingly as a sacrifice.

The ox in the Temple and the stall
Infancy and beginnings, Luke 1–4.13

Since the ox was the universal beast of burden, it is not sur-prising that Luke stresses the universal importance of Jesus. We have seen that the opening words of any ancient text were crucial. If Mark is not concerned with the origins of his Jesus bounding on to the stage, while Matthew locates him firmly in Israel's history, Luke's opening has a very different feel. His preface (1.1–4) is a single Greek sentence, beautifully balanced around the author's intention: 'I too decided'. Verses 1–2 reflect back on previous accounts, while vv.3–4 look ahead to his book. The author writes self-consciously in the first person to someone with a Greek name, Theophilus ('Lover of God'), and an official title, 'your Excellency'. We don't know who he was, but such dedications to a publisher or benefactor were typical in Graeco-Roman writings. Luke has moved Jesus' biography on to the universal stage as a Graeco-Roman 'life', and similar prefaces can be found in many other ancient biographies. His account is a 'narrative' (*diegesis*) which will be 'in sequence' or 'orderly' (*kathexes*); this does not necessarily mean chronological order, since in Acts 11.4 Peter tells his story 'in order' (*kathexes*), but in a different sequence from that in Acts 10. As Peter tells his story from his perspective, so also the evangelist will narrate his gospel. We must discover Luke's perspective and read his narrative, *diegesis*, to uncover his portrait of Jesus the bearer of burdens.

Many ancient lives have opening stories before the main narrative about the subject's background and family, his birth or infancy, and perhaps a little vignette of childhood or education—all carefully chosen to introduce the main themes of the life to follow. Such themes would recur throughout the narrative and come to a climax at the end. In Greek drama, the prologue prepared the audience for the action, which was summed up in the epilogue at the end. Similarly, an overture familiarizes the waiting audience with the themes of the ballet or opera to follow. In his opening stories, Luke begins his portrait of Jesus as a bearer of burdens, among the poor and lowly, at prayer and in the Temple—and yet with universal implications.

Unlike Mark's breathless dashing lion, Luke's ox plods along slowly. To understand Jesus, we go back beyond the adult Jesus' baptism (as in Mark) and even beyond his birth (as in Matthew), to the childless parents of his forerunner— and it all takes two long chapters! Remarkably, the style changes from the quasi-classical Greek of the preface to an Old Testament atmosphere. Luke is a writer with literary skill; changes of style happen throughout the gospel—and on into Acts, where a gradual linguistic shift from a Semitic style to more cosmopolitan Greek mirrors the geographical shift from Jerusalem to Rome. In these opening stories, phrases like 'the house of', 'before the face of', 'and behold', 'and it came to pass' evoke the Hebrew scriptures. Zechariah and Elizabeth are 'righteous before God' (like Noah, Gen. 6.9) and childless (like Abraham and Sarah, Gen. 16.1; 18.11); they burst into psalms of praise (like Moses and Miriam in Exod.15.1–21, or Hannah in 1 Sam.

2.1–10). There are angels and miraculous births, and Simeon and Anna keep the ancient faith alive in the Temple. This is Luke's overture's first theme: Jesus comes out of Israel's history.

Unlike Matthew's kings, wise men, and the powerful, Luke begins with the ox, among the pious poor and women, the meek and the lowly—Zechariah and Elizabeth, and Mary herself. While Matthew sees things through Joseph's eyes, Luke takes Mary's viewpoint, treasured in her heart (2.19, 51); the opening chapter is not about his genealogy, but her family. The angel appears not in a dream to Joseph (Matt. 1.20), but visibly to Mary (Lk. 1.26), her kinsman (1.11) and to the shepherds (2.9). Those who bear the burdens of this world praise God in the revolutionary tones of the Magnificat (1.46–55) and Benedictus (1.68–79) for his salvation for the poor and overthrow of the powerful. When Jesus is finally born, he is laid in an ox's feeding trough because 'there was no place for them at the inn' (2.7). In this way, a second theme enters Luke's music, a quiet motif scored for the lower instruments.

However, the ox may look gentle, but it is powerful to work great things. There are four outbursts of joy and praise at what God is doing: Elizabeth and Mary's delight (1.41–56); the wondrous birth of John the Baptist (1.58, 63–80); the angels and the shepherds (2.10–20); Simeon and Anna (2.28–38)—leading to John's preaching (3.1–6). Each one picks up the themes and develops them: joy (1.14, 47; 2.10) in preparing the way (1.17, 76; 3.4) for the coming Davidic King (1.32–3, 69–71; 2.11) who is Saviour, bringing salvation (1.47, 69, 71, 77; 2.11, 30; 3.6), mercy and forgiveness (1.50, 54, 72, 77, 78; 3.3) and peace (1.79; 2.14, 29) from Abraham and the prophets (1.54–55, 69–70) to all peoples (2.31–32; 3.6). So like some fugue, phrase after phrase is tossed around from one song to another, building to a crescendo of all Luke's ideas about the coming of Jesus.

As the ox was often found in the Temple for sacrifice, so too, the poor are welcome before God. The gospel begins with a righteous priest, Zechariah, in the Temple (1.5–23). Jesus himself is taken to the Temple when only a few weeks old for his mother's purification (2.22–24). Mary and Joseph redeem him by two pigeons (2.24), the offering permitted to those too poor for the normal cost of a lamb and a pigeon (Lev. 12.6–8). Despite this socio-economic background, Jesus is recognized in the Temple by Simeon and Anna who praise God for his salvation (2.22–38).

Luke alone includes a typical biographical childhood story foreshadowing the adult. The boy Jesus confounding the wise teachers reminds us of the early brilliance of Cicero at school (Plutarch, *Cicero*, II.2)—but this is also in the Temple (2.41–51). While Matthew concludes both the temptation narrative (Matt. 4.8) and his gospel itself (28.16) on mountains, Luke has the temptation about the kingdoms of the world second in his sequence and there is no mountain (Lk. 4.5). The final temptation takes place in Jerusalem (which only Luke names) in the Temple (4.9); and, in another 'bookend' or framing device, Luke ends his gospel also in Jerusalem in the Temple (24.53). 'The ox knows its owner' (Is. 1.3)—and Jesus must be in his Father's house (Lk. 2.49).

Yet, despite the Semitic language and Jewish atmosphere, the final theme depicts the universal implications of Jesus. If Luke's Jesus is the ox, the bearer of burdens of the lowly poor and women, this also includes the Gentiles. The child is called Jesus, Saviour (1.31)—but he is for *universal* salvation, and his birth is located in the events of world history (2.1–2). Although the shepherds are told of the Saviour's birth in the city of David (2.11), the heavenly choir sings of peace and God's gracious favour to all on earth (2.14). The emperor Augustus was called 'Saviour of the world' on monuments, and he was renowned for closing the doors of the Temple of War at Rome. The true Saviour and bringer of peace, according to Luke, is to be found in an ox's shed behind a pub in a provincial backwater! Simeon, paragon of Old Testament piety, recognizes that Jesus is not just for himself and for Israel, but also 'a light for revelation to the Gentiles', 'prepared in the presence of all peoples' (2.29–32); he warns Mary that this child will bring division for 'many in Israel' (2.34). While Matthew and Mark apply

Isaiah's voice crying in the wilderness to John the Baptist, only Luke continues that 'all peoples shall see the salvation of God' (3.6, quoting Is. 40.5). Again, he locates his story in both Roman and Jewish history and rulers (3.1–2). Finally, while Matthew begins with the genealogy from Abraham to Joseph, Luke places it after the baptism as Jesus begins his public ministry: he takes his genealogy of seventy-seven names back past Abraham and Jewish patriarchs to Adam, son of God and father of the whole human race (3.38) thus bringing to a climax his overture's final theme of Jesus as universal Saviour.

Thus, like an overture before a play or opera, Luke's opening stories of the ox in the Temple and the stall introduce the main themes of his gospel. Jesus comes from a Jewish background of the pious poor, always welcome before God in the Temple. Yet, the horns of the ox work great and mighty acts—and nothing less than God's universal salvation is happening here.

The ox plods a long, slow journey *Luke's style and structure*

Unlike Mark's disorderly rushing about, Luke writes an 'orderly account' (1.4). His preface has a calm, literary self-confidence, and this continues into the main narrative. While Mark introduces everything 'and immediately', Luke prefers the more leisurely 'and it came to pass' (e.g. 3.21; 5.1, 12, 17; 9.18, 51), sometimes adding 'in those days' (2.1; 6.12). 'And it came to pass' is a Greek translation of the Hebrew *wayehi*, used by Matthew six times, Mark four times, John three times and the rest of the New Testament only twice. Luke, however, has it no less than fifty times in his gospel and a further fifteen times in Acts: in a steady plodding pace, the ox puts one foot in front of another, as things 'come to pass' and event follows event.

While half of Matthew comes from Mark, with a quarter shared with Luke ('Q') and a quarter unique ('M'), Luke's mixture is rather different: about 29 per cent of his text follows Mark and 13 per cent comes from 'Q', while about

43 per cent is his own special material ('L'), with the remaining 15 per cent mixing two or three sources. Furthermore, his order shows an interesting oscillation between Mark and the others:

Luke	Mark as source	Q and L material
1.1–3.2		is unique = L
3.3–4.30	mixes Mark 1.1–20	with Q and L.
4.31–6.19	follows basically Mark 1.21–3.19	
6.20–8.3		combines Q and L
8.4–9.50	follows basically Mk. 4.1–9.40	
9.51–18.14		combines Q and L
18.15–24.12	Mark 10.13–16.8	with L material inserted through Passion
24.12–50		is unique = L

This oscillation is understandable given that the gospels, like other ancient books, were written on scrolls about ten metres long. To get to my desk, I have to pick my way through over a hundred books strewn around my study, open at different pages for easy reference; the ancient writer would only have had room for one scroll before him as he worked. Basically, Matthew follows Mark all the time and

probably has a copy open on his desk; to portray Jesus as
the Teacher of Israel, he inserts the other material in his
five great sermons into the flow of Mark's narrative. Luke
seems to have Mark open before him when he is writing
3.3–6.19, 8.4–9.50 and 18.15–24.12; at other times, he
probably rolled up Mark, preferring to combine Q with
material gathered from his own sources (L). This special
material reflects his particular concerns for the poor, women
and Gentiles, for prayer and joy. He does not collect non-
Markan stuff into sermons like Matthew, but interweaves
deeds and sayings, often with his own setting or story (L)
leading to teaching shared with Matthew (Q). Thus, he
portrays Jesus as someone who teaches not just by word,
but also by action, earthing what he says in what he does.
The ox is, above all things, a worker.

Luke's structure is carefully designed with a geographical dimension. Unlike Mark's bounding lion rushing
around all over the place, Luke's ox moves very deliberately
towards his goal. After the opening stories in Jerusalem and
the Temple (1.5–4.13), we have Jesus' ministry in Galilee
(4.14–9.50), concluding with his deliberate decision to 'set
his face to go to Jerusalem' (9.51). It is a long and steady
journey (9.51–19.27) full of Luke's own material ('L'), with
Jerusalem repeatedly mentioned (9.53; 13.22, 33–4; 17.11;
18.31; 19.11, 28). There is no mistaking where this ox
is headed. Jerusalem is named about thirty-three times in
Luke's gospel, as often as in Matthew, Mark and John
combined; while it comes sixty times in Acts, the rest of the
New Testament has it only fourteen times, which shows
how central it is in Luke's thinking. The ox goes to Jerusalem to be sacrificed: only Luke points out that 'it cannot
be that a prophet should perish away from Jerusalem'
(13.33). Significantly, the risen Jesus instructs the disciples
to 'stay here in the city' (24.49), where they go to the
Temple again (24.53); there is no command to go back to
Matthew's mountains in Galilee. In Luke's second book,
Jerusalem is the base from which the church spreads out
into the whole world and on to Rome itself (Acts 1.8).

Not only do we have geography, but history too. Unlike

Mark's enigmatic lack of information about his bounding lion, Luke places his Jesus carefully with full dating (2.1–2; 3.1–2). Recent studies of Luke have shown that Jesus stands in 'the Middle of Time', the pivot around whom all history centres, the time of fulfilment. Before Jesus, there is the past, the time of prophecy in the Jewish scriptures; after Jesus, there is the future, the period of the church which Luke will describe in the book of Acts. The gospel is carefully structured historically, from the deliberate Old Testament feel of the opening chapters, through to the disciples in Jerusalem at the end beginning the church, and on into the second volume, the Acts of the Apostles. Luke has a flow of events, symbolized by the steady progress of the ox.

Furthermore, Luke demonstrates through this flow that the Christians are the true heirs of Israel, using Old Testament motifs and allusions to divine knowledge and plan. The little word *dei*, 'it is necessary', occurs as often in Luke as in the other gospels combined (e.g. 2.49; 4.43; 9.22; 11.42; 13.14, 16; 15.32; 19.5; 21.9; 22.7, 37). The risen Jesus explains that 'it was necessary' for all the scriptures and prophecies to be fulfilled in him (24.26–7, 44). Unlike Mark's frantic pace leading to the immediate End of all things (Mk. 13.5–37), Luke's Jesus is more measured. For Luke 'the end will not be immediately' (Lk. 21.9, contrast Mk. 13.7); to those who expect the kingdom of God 'immediately', Luke's Jesus tells the parable of the king going away and giving his servants ten pounds each to use for him (19.11–27). It is all less urgent, and there is more affirmation of the world: the Roman empire is not a Satanic evil (as in Revelation), but protects Christians as the gospel spreads in Acts. The 'dawn from on high' has already broken in with the births of John and Jesus (1.78). Luke omits Mark and Matthew's announcement that 'the Kingdom of God is at hand' (Mk. 1.15; Matt. 4.17). Instead, 'today' is born the Saviour (2.11); Jesus proclaims that 'today' the scriptures announcing the Lord's favour are fulfilled (4.21), 'today' salvation comes to a tax gatherer like Zacchaeus (19.9) and 'today' Paradise is open even to a repentant thief (23.43).

The progress of the ox may be slow—but it is also sure and steady through time and space, geography and history.

The ox, the herd, and the drivers   *Luke's characterization*

The gospels' stories involve three main protagonists—Jesus himself, his disciples and the religious leaders of his day, with three storylines developing *en route* to their shared climax at the death and resurrection. So let us now consider Jesus as the ox, his herd of disciples and the religious leaders who are supposed to tend their cattle.

Jesus

Luke's view of Jesus stresses his humanity, with his lowly family background, birth and boyhood. When our children were small, my wife and I took great delight in charting their progress in baby development books. Luke alone records the child development of both John the Baptist (1.80) and of the infant Jesus (2.40): 'Jesus grew in wisdom and in stature, and in favour with God and people' (2.52). It does not reflect well on a family if they think their son is crazy, so Luke completely omits the family's attempt to restrain Jesus (Mk. 3.21, linked to the Beelzebul controversy in Mk. 3.19–35), and moves their desire to see him (Lk. 8.19–21) away from the Beelzebul debate (Lk. 11.14–23). Like Matthew, Luke also omits Mark's comments about Jesus' ignorance (such as Mk. 13.32, or Mk. 15.34) and passes over the references to his human feelings (e.g. pity in Mk. 1.41: Lk. 5.13; anger Mk. 3.5: Lk. 6.10; indignation Mk. 10.14: Lk. 18.16).

Throughout the first part of Jesus' ministry, Luke constantly raises questions about Jesus' identity. Worshippers wonder in the synagogues of Nazareth (4.22) and Capernaum (4.36); questions are asked by the scribes and Pharisees (5.21), John the Baptist (7.19), the disciples (8.25) and Herod (9.9). Jesus questions his disciples and Peter confesses him as 'the Christ of God' (9.18–22): Luke does not say where this event took place and is much briefer than Matthew (omitting Peter and the church, Matt. 16.17–19) and Mark (omitting Peter's protests and Jesus' rebuke, Mk. 8.32–33). While this event is the pivot of Mark's gospel, Luke's first key change comes later, when Jesus sets his face to Jerusalem (9.51). Rather than Mark's climactic moment of revelation at Caesarea Philippi, Luke provides several suggestions for Jesus' identity.

The first answer is to see Jesus as a prophet. The baptism scene in Luke reminds us of a prophetic anointing; John the Baptist and Matthew's conversation about righteousness is missing, while Luke stresses the descent of the Holy Spirit and the voice addressed to Jesus, 'You are my beloved Son' (3.21–22). Equally, the prophetic atmosphere of Jesus' rejection at Nazareth is enhanced by the references to Elijah and Elisha (4.16–30). The raising of the widow's son at Nain recalls Elijah's similar miracle (Lk. 7.11–17, cp. 1 Kings 17.17–24). Further, the crowd call Jesus 'a great prophet' (7.16), which is questioned by Simon the Pharisee (7.39). Both those around Herod (9.8) and the disciples suggest that people see Jesus as a prophet (9.19). Jesus compares himself with Jonah (11.29–32) and the rejection and murder of prophets (11.47–52); he calls himself a prophet at Nazareth (4.24) and he makes a prophetic journey to the holy city because 'it cannot be that a prophet should perish away from Jerusalem' (13.33). No wonder that after his death, he is called 'a prophet mighty in deed and word' by a disciple, Cleopas, on the way to Emmaus (24.19). Elsewhere, Jesus uses 'Son of Man' to designate himself in front of Pharisees (5.21–24; 6.1–5), disciples (6.20–22) or crowds (7.24, 34). As in the other gospels, this does not reveal his identity so much as indicate his activity; he is 'the man' who suffers (7.34; 9.22, 44) and who will come in judgement to be vindicated by God (9.26; 11.30; 18.8; 21.27).

Luke's own answer reveals a rich christology. First, the angel announces that there is born 'in the city of David, a Saviour, who is Christ the Lord' (2.11). The only synoptic evangelist to use this title, Luke calls God 'my Saviour' (1.47), and then applies the same term to Jesus (2.11). Jesus tells people that their faith has 'saved' them (7.50; 17.19; 18.42); salvation comes to Zacchaeus, because 'the Son of Man came to seek and save the lost' (19.9–10). The angel's reference to the city of David recalls God's promise to David's line (2 Sam. 7.8–16); Mary is told that Jesus will receive 'the throne of his father David' (1.32–33). Simeon sees Jesus as 'the Lord's Christ' (2.26) and Peter agrees in his confession of 'the Christ of God' (9.20); Jesus is accused of calling himself 'Christ the king' (23.2; see also 19.38; 23.35, 37–39, 42) and refers to himself after his resurrection, 'that the Christ should suffer these things and enter into his glory' (24.26).

In his inaugural sermon, Jesus quotes Isaiah that 'the Lord has anointed [literally, *christ*-ed] me' (4.18). While the other gospel writers depict Jesus being addressed as *kyrie*, this means just a deferential lord, sir, or master; they never refer to Jesus by the full title in his lifetime. Only Luke uses the definite term 'the Lord' for Jesus in his actual narrative: first it refers to God in narrative comments fourteen times in the first five chapters (1.6, 9, 11, 58, 66; 2.9, 22, 23a–b, 24, 26, 39; 3.4; 5.17), then a further fourteen times to refer to Jesus (7.13, 19; 10.1, 39, 41; 11.39; 12.42; 13.15; 17.5, 6; 18.6; 19.8; 22.61; 24.34). As God is 'the Lord', so too is Jesus. Given the gospels' caution about using post-Easter affirmations of faith for the human Jesus, this shift in Luke is indicative of his own view: Jesus is 'the Lord', the Son of God, as the angel announces (1.32, 35) and the voice confirms (3.22; 9.35); demons recognize this also (4.34, 41; 8.28) and it is accepted by Jesus at his trial (22.70).

The ox is a powerful and mighty creature, the king of domestic beasts, and yet a sacrificial victim. There is no Markan secret here in Luke. John the Baptist is a prophet, and Jesus has much of the prophet about him; but he is also the Davidic Messiah, the Son of God, Saviour, and the Lord. As such, Jesus calls Israel to repentance, but in this gospel rejection begins at home (4.16–30). While Jesus' identity as Son of God is clear to supernatural beings, human responses differ: some see him as a prophet, others as a false Messiah, while for the disciples he is Christ the Lord. As Simeon warned, he creates division for 'the fall and rising of many in Israel' (2.34). To these we must now turn.

Those who follow behind the ox

When Elijah called Elisha, he found him ploughing behind twelve yoke of oxen (1 Kings 19.19). Luke is interested in those who plough behind his ox—but the yokes are not limited to twelve. Luke is comparatively less interested in the disciples as a distinct group (the term occurs only thirty-seven times, half as often as in Matthew or John)—but is more interested in people's reactions to Jesus. He has more personal names and realistic details of people such as Zechariah and Elizabeth (1.5–80), Simon the Pharisee and the woman sinner (7.36–50), or Zacchaeus (19.1–10). Luke is more positive about the large crowds with Jesus (3.21; 11.29; 12.1; 23.5); Jesus was popular as they welcome him (8.40), rejoice at what he does (13.17), and hang on his words (19.48; 21.38). Luke alone says that Judas had to betray him away from the crowd (22.6) and he depicts a great multitude following Jesus to the cross wailing and lamenting (23.27).

Thus, the formation of Jesus' followers is wider than just the twelve. The call of Peter and the others takes place *after* Jesus' initial preaching (4.16–32, 42–44), exorcisms and healings (4.33–41); Luke's unique story of the miraculous catch of fish explains why Peter and his colleagues left everything to follow him (5.1–11). Luke calls a much larger group 'disciples', out of which Jesus chose twelve 'apostles' (6.13). The twelve are sent out on mission practice (9.1–6, cp. Matt. 10.1, 5) but only Luke tells us also of another seventy (or seventy-two in some manuscripts) being sent out in pairs (10.1–16). Only Luke mentions women disciples: he names Mary Magdalene (and the seven demons cast from her), Joanna the wife of Herod's steward Chuza, Susanna, and many others, who provided financial support for the disciples (8.1–3). In his unique story of Mary and Martha, Martha has a traditional view of the woman's place being in the kitchen: Jesus' acceptance of Mary as a disciple at his feet is radical indeed (10.38–42).

The twelve are seen in a better light: from Mark's depiction of them with no faith, to Matthew's 'little faith', in Luke they actually ask Jesus, 'Increase our faith' (17.5, cp. Matt. 17.20). Luke omits Mark's criticisms of the disciples (compare, for example, Mk. 4.13 with Lk. 8.11) and their questions (Mk. 9.10: Lk. 9.37); while in Matthew James' and John's request for the good seats in heaven is made by their mother, Luke omits it in tactful silence (Mk. 10.35–45: Matt. 20.20)! As for the inner threesome, Luke explains their panic at the transfiguration as arising from their tiredness and fear (Lk. 9.32–4); in Gethsemane, he does not single out Peter, James and John, and excuses the *one* sleep (not Mark's *three*) of *all* the disciples as being 'for sorrow' (22.45). Mark's 'they all forsook him and fled' is omitted (Mk. 14.50, cp. Lk. 22.53); instead 'all his acquaintances and the women' witness the crucifixion 'from a distance' (Lk. 23.49). However, it is not all positive: they did not understand about humility at the Last Supper (22.24–7), or non-violence in the garden (22.35–38, 49–50). After the resurrection Jesus still has to explain things to Cleopas (24.25–7, 32) and the others before they can receive the 'power from on high' (24.46–9).

Instead of following Jesus for no apparent reason (as in Mk. 1.16–18), Simon Peter first witnesses both the healing of his mother-in-law (Lk. 4.38–39) and the miraculous catch of fish (5.1–11), responding with awe: 'depart from me, for I am a sinful man, O Lord' (5.8). None the less, Jesus makes him his co-worker, the first named when the twelve are chosen (6.14); as elsewhere, he is the spokesman, confessing Jesus as Christ (9.20), madly offering to build booths at the transfiguration (9.33) and pointing out their commitment in leaving everything to follow Jesus (18.28). Luke omits Peter's protests about Jesus' prediction of his passion and Jesus' rebuke (cp. Lk. 9.22 with Mk. 8.32–33), nor does Jesus complain that not even Peter could stay awake in Gethsemane (cp. Lk. 22.40–46 with Mk. 14.33, 37). Instead of Peter's rash promise not to desert (Mk. 14.29–31), in Luke, Jesus prophesies Peter's denial at the Last Supper; Satan is behind it, but Jesus has prayed for Peter's faith not to fail utterly, and when he has turned again, he is to strengthen his 'brethren' (Lk. 22.31–34). 'Brethren' is used regularly by Luke for the Christians in Acts where Peter is their leader (e.g. Acts 1.15; 15.7, 23). Even at Peter's denial, he omits the cursing or swearing (cp. Lk. 22.60 with Mk. 14.71); instead, only Luke says that 'the Lord turned and looked at Peter; and Peter remembered' (22.61)—and he alone tells us of an appearance of the risen Christ to Peter (24.34). The ox plods a long but steady journey, out beyond death and resurrection to the Acts of the Apostles, led initially by Peter. The stories of Peter, Stephen and Paul will repeat the trials and sufferings of the sacrificial ox. Again, Luke's account is part of the flow of history.

The religious leaders

Mark's lion was in conflict with both the natural and supernatural worlds, while Matthew's Teacher of Israel was rejected by her leaders. Luke, however, begins with a priest, Zechariah in the Temple (1.5–23); Simeon and Anna, devout worshippers in the Temple, recognize the infant Saviour (2.22–38); thirdly, also in the Temple the twelve-year old Jesus first encounters religious teachers—and they are amazed (2.41–51). So we begin with positive feelings about the Temple and religious leaders. None the less, the Magnificat warns of the overthrow of the powerful (1.51–52) and Simeon prophesied division for 'many in Israel' (2.34). During Jesus' ministry in Galilee (4.14–9.50) and his journey to Jerusalem (9.51–19.27), the Pharisees appear regularly to debate with Jesus about tradition and the law: they question his authority to forgive (5.21–2; 7.49), fasting (5.33–39), activity and healing on the sabbath (6.1–2, 6–11; 13.14; 14.1–6), purity (11.38), and complain about Jesus' keeping company with sinners (5.29–32; 7.39; 15.1–2). The debate between the twelve-year-old and the leaders is

continuing in Jesus' ministry, and it is not yet confronta-
tional: only Luke depicts Pharisees inviting Jesus to dinner
for discussions between equals. Thus, Luke's unique story
of the dinner with Simon the Pharisee allows extravagant
love to be shown to Jesus by the forgiven woman sinner
(7.36–50).

Luke uses another dinner with a Pharisee for the Q
teaching on inner and outer purity found in Matthew's great
diatribe (cp. Lk. 11.37–44 with Matt. 23.6–7, 23, 25–27).
Discussion with lawyers, scribes and Pharisees (11.45, 53;
12.1) uses more of Matthew's sermon (cp. Lk. 11.45–12.1
with Matt. 23. 4, 29–31, 34–36, 13). Thus, instead of a
single discourse like Matthew 23, here Jesus' criticism
emerges in conversation. Rather than plotting with the
Herodians (Mk. 3.6), some Pharisees warn him that 'Herod
wants to kill you' (Lk. 13.31). A further dinner debate
with Pharisees about healing on the sabbath provides more
teaching on humility, the parable of the messianic supper,
and discipleship (14.1–35). Despite all these dinner parties,
Jesus still has to defend eating with sinners by telling the
Pharisees the parables of the lost sheep, coin, and prodigal
son (15.1–3); Luke calls them 'lovers of money' who
scoffed (16.14). A self-righteous Pharisee is contrasted with
the repentant tax-collector in the unique parable of 18.9–14,
but, after a brief protest about the crowd's reaction to Jesus'
entry into Jerusalem (19.39), the Pharisees disappear, not
mentioned again until the book of Acts.

Jesus' demonstration in the Temple and his 'teaching
daily' there provokes the first serious danger: 'the chief
priests, the scribes and the leaders of the people sought to
destroy him' (19.45–47). The conflict is no longer with
Pharisees over dinner, but with powerful leaders who control the sacrificial system—and who know how to handle an
ox which will not stay in its stall! None the less, they have
to be careful, since the ordinary people were spellbound
by Jesus' words (19.48). Jesus' activity in the Temple is
perceived as a direct challenge, so the chief priests, scribes,
and elders question him about his authority (20.1–8). A
dangerous game of cat and mouse ensues to force Jesus

either to offend the crowd or to get him into trouble with the Romans. Jesus replies with his counter-question about the authority of John the Baptist; only Luke says that the priests were frightened that 'all the people will stone us' (20.6). The parable of the tenants of the vineyard is told against them but they can do nothing for fear of the crowd (20.9–19). As in Mark and Matthew, questions about taxes to Caesar (20.20–26) and the resurrection (20.27–40) follow, but from chief priests, scribes, and elders (20.20) rather than Pharisees and Herodians (Mk. 12.13; Matt. 22.15–16). After this, 'they no longer dared to ask him any question' (20.40).

Instead of the question about the greatest commandment, already included earlier together with his unique parable of the Good Samaritan (10.25–28, 29–37), Luke continues with the questions about David's son (20.41–44), and a brief denunciation of the scribes (20.45–47, rather than Matthew's diatribe against the Pharisees, Matt. 23). Luke's brief eschatological teaching prophesies the destruction of the Temple (21.5–36), but omits the Mount of Olives (Mk. 13.3; Matt. 24.3). The conflict is a stalemate: while Jesus teaches daily in the Temple to those who gather early to hear him (21. 37–38), the chief priests and scribes can do nothing because 'they feared the people' (22.2). Only in Luke does Satan now intervene, inspiring Judas Iscariot to betray Jesus 'in the absence of the crowd' (22.3–6). After his arrest, Jesus is brought to the high priest's house (22.54), from where the chief priests, elders and scribes take him to Pilate (22.66–23.2). Only Luke recounts a hearing and mocking before Herod (23.6–11), but eventually he and Pilate both declare that Jesus has done 'nothing deserving death' and they propose to release him (23.12–16). Luke stresses that it is the chief priests and the scribes who accuse him 'vehemently' (23.10), hear Pilate's decision (23.13) and protest so strongly that he finally delivers him 'up to their will' (23.25).

Thus, Luke's three-part geographical structure of Galilee –Journey–Jerusalem develops the conflict essential to his story. After the opening positive feeling about the Temple and religious leaders, the Pharisees in the Galilee and Journey sections are Jesus' debating partners and dinner hosts. However, in the Jerusalem chapters they are replaced by the chief priests and elders—much more dangerous opponents who are ultimately responsible for Jesus' death. Instead of being leaders caring for the herd, they only know how to butcher the ox. Luke and his Gentile church are not in debate with rabbinic Pharisaism like Matthew. In the Acts of the Apostles, the Pharisees reappear in a good light: Gamaliel speaks up for the early Christians (5.34); some believers are Pharisees (15.5) and Paul uses his Pharisaic background (23.6–9; 26.5). For Luke's picture of Jesus the bearer of burdens, the real opponents are the rich and powerful who control the Temple, not for the humble poor, but for their own advantage. Their apparently successful slaughter of the ox will actually bring down the powerful and lift up the lowly, as prophesied in the Magnificat (1.52). This must be our next concern.

Those who are burdened with heavy loads
The ministry of the ox

The keynote for Luke's portrait of Jesus is set in his initial visit to the synagogue at Nazareth (4.16–30). Luke's story is three times longer than the equivalent accounts which occur much later in Mark and Matthew (Mk. 6.1–6; Matt. 13.54–58). It is the crucial curtain-raiser for the rest of Jesus' ministry. Luke shows Jesus fulfilling Isaiah's prophecy, anointed by the Spirit to preach good news to the poor and release to the captives, blind and oppressed (4.18–21), instead of 'Repent, the Kingdom of God is at hand' (Mk. 1.15; Matt. 4.17). For Luke, Jesus is the ox, the bearer of burdens for the poor and all in need. The congregation is initially impressed with the local boy making good (4.22), until he mentions Elijah and Elisha's ministry to the Gentiles, the widow of Sidon and Naaman the Syrian (4.26–27). This concern for the burdens of all, for universal salvation, leads to an angry rejection of Jesus. He is not just an impressive young man, but a prophet escaping death, as 'he journeyed on'. *Poreuomai* is one of Luke's favourite words, as Jesus 'journeys on' through deserts (4.42) and towns (7.11), to Jerusalem (9.51, 53; 13.33; 17.11; 19.28) for his destiny (22.22); after his resurrection he will 'journey' with disciples to Emmaus (24.13, 28). Luke's gospel is the journey of salvation; the ox bears the burdens of the poor, the captives and the blind, the oppressed and widows, as it travels beyond local and national concerns to the Gentiles to declare 'the year of the Lord's favour' (4.19).

Rich and poor

We saw that the ox was a symbol of wealth (Prov. 14.4) and Proverbs contrasts a poor 'dinner of vegetables' with a fatted ox as a symbol of luxury (Prov. 15.17). Although Luke is often called the 'gospel for the poor', he has many warnings to the rich: only Luke comments that a person's life 'does not consist in abundant possessions' and the parable of the rich fool (12.13–21) reinforces Jesus' teaching, 'sell your possessions' (12.22–34). Similarly, the unique parable of the rich man and Lazarus, told to the Pharisees as 'lovers of money' (16.14), shows the rich man punished for his selfishness (16.19–31). Mark and Matthew's young man was told to 'sell' his 'great possessions' (Mk. 10.17–31; Matt. 19.16–30); in Luke he is 'very rich' and Jesus instructs him to 'sell *all* you have' (18.18–25). Zacchaeus, who appears only in Luke, is also called 'rich' (19.2), but unlike the young man (18.23), he does what Jesus says: 'today salvation has come to this house' (19.1–10).

This fulfils the Magnificat's putting down of the mighty and sending away of the rich; the other side of the great reversal was exalting the lowly and filling the hungry with good things (1.52–53). So, it is the poor to whom Jesus preaches good news (4.18; 7.22); it is the poor and the hungry who are blessed in Luke's Beatitude (6.20–21, unlike Matthew's 'poor in spirit' and 'those who hunger for righteousness', Matt. 5.3, 6), and the corresponding Woes to the rich are unique to Luke (6.24–26). The poor Lazarus is now comforted in Abraham's bosom (16.25). Only in

Luke does Jesus tell people not to invite the rich to dinner, but the 'poor, maimed and blind' (14.12–14); his version of the parable of the messianic supper follows immediately in which the 'poor, maimed and blind' are brought in after the rich possessors of fields, oxen, and wives have refused the invitation (14.15–24, contrast Matthew's inclusion of 'good and bad', Matt. 22.9–10).

The lost and the unacceptable

As well as dining with Pharisees, Luke's Jesus eats with 'sinners' (5.29–32; 15.1–2; 19.7), a word more frequent in Luke than in the other three gospels combined. Peter calls himself a sinner when he meets Jesus (5.8), but fortunately Jesus is 'a friend of sinners' (7.34); only Luke says that there will be more joy in heaven over one repentant sinner than ninety-nine righteous (15.7). True to his opening manifesto (4.18–19), Jesus consorts with lepers (5.12–16; 7.22; 17.11–19), the crippled (5.17–26; 7.22), the blind (7.21–22; 18.35–43) and tax-collectors (5.27–30; 15.1–2; 19.1–10). Normally, these people would all be unacceptable in society, excluded from meals and from worship out of fear of impurity. In response to the Pharisees' criticism, we have three parables of the lost to justify Jesus' behaviour (15:1–32). The parable of the lost sheep also occurs in Matthew with the hypothetical '*if* he finds it' (18.13); for Luke this is a certainty, '*when* he has found it'—and then there is a party (15.5)! Only Luke contains the parables of the lost coin (15.8–10) and the lost or prodigal son (15.11–32), the longest parable in the gospels, full of narrative detail and characterization; the Lukan reversal of rich and poor leads to the dramatic reversal of the father from desolation to joy, of the younger son from death to life, and the elder son from happiness to jealousy. Finally, we notice the party once again—including a fatted calf, the young of the ox!

Women

Also socially less acceptable were women; Martha points out that they should be serving the men (10.40). Luke begins with stories about Elizabeth, Anna and Mary. While Mary appears occasionally elsewhere (Mk. 3.31–35; 6.3; Matt. 1.16–20; 2.11; 13.53), Luke calls her by name thirteen times (1.27, 30, 34, 38, 39, 41, 46, 56; 2.5, 16, 19, 34; Acts 1.14) and also refers to her in 2.41–51; 8.19–21; 11.27–28. Luke has many unique incidents involving women: the widow of Nain (7.11–17); the woman with ointment (7.36–50); the support of women disciples (8.2–3); Mary's right to sit and listen to Jesus (10.38–42); a woman in the crowd (11.27); the woman healed on the sabbath (13.10–17). In addition to these found only in Luke, he includes from Mark Peter's mother-in-law (4.38–39), Jairus' daughter and the woman with the haemorrhage (8.41–56). Women also feature regularly in Luke's parables, often paired with a man: the woman with leaven follows the man with a mustard seed (13.18–21); a woman's lost coin pairs the man's lost sheep (15.3–10); the two women grinding, one taken at the End and one left, balance the two men in bed, one taken and one left (17.34–35). Thus, Luke portrays Jesus being inclusive in his teaching. He is also concerned for widows: Anna, the widowed prophetess in the Temple (2.37); the widow of Sidon (4.25–26); the widow of Nain (7.12); the poor widow offering her all (21.1–4, the only widow in the other gospels, Mk. 12.41–44). A widow provides an example of persistent prayer in Luke's unique parable (18.1–8). With no one to care for them, they were very vulnerable and Luke shows them receiving special care also in the early church (Acts 6.1; 9.39–41).

Non-Jews

The bearer of burdens is concerned also for non-Jews. A good Samaritan, one of the mixed race of Israelites and Assyrians shunned by Jews since the Exile, shows true love of neighbour, while the priest and Levite pass by in Luke's special parable (10.29–37). Similarly, the only one of ten lepers who returns to thank Jesus for his healing is a Samaritan in a story unique to Luke (17.11–19). Luke's concern for universal salvation was foreshadowed in Simeon's praise for the 'revelation to the Gentiles' (2.32) and Elijah and Elisha's ministry to non-Jews (4.24–27). Only Luke shows Jesus refusing James' and John's hot-headed request to bring fire down on the Samaritans (9.51–6). Luke repeats the stories of Gentiles found in the other gospels: the centurion with faith like none in Israel (7.1–10, cp. Matt. 8.5–13); the Gerasene demoniac (8.26–39, cp. Mk. 5.1–20); the men of Nineveh and Queen of the South (11.29–32, cp. Matt. 12.38–42); the warnings of the parables of the messianic supper (14.15–24, cp. Matt. 22.1–10), and the vineyard (20.9–19, cp. Matt. 21.33–46). Luke's interest in history looks ahead to what he uniquely terms 'the times of the Gentiles' (21.24); the mission to all nations concludes this gospel (24.47)—and leads to the framing 'bookends' of his second volume (Acts 1.8 and 28.28).

As the ox was the universal ancient carrier of heavy loads, so Luke portrays Jesus as concerned for all those bearing burdens, especially those who have none to share the weight—the poor, outcasts, women, and Gentiles. The ox plods its steady journey to Jerusalem, and picks up more and more burdens as it goes—but where does it get the energy this requires?

Strength to bear the burdens   *Luke's spirituality*

As well as a patient steady plodder, carrying heavy loads, the ox was a very religious symbol for Jews, being used for sacrifice, and its horns representing the power of God. If Luke is the evangelist who depicts Jesus as the bearer of burdens, he also most clearly describes his resources.

Prayer

This gospel opens with prayer in the Temple (1.5–23) and it also closes with the disciples 'continually in the Temple blessing God' (24.53). Luke's Jesus is nothing, if not a man of prayer. Time after time, Luke makes special mention of Jesus being at prayer when things happen—at his baptism (3.21), after ministry to others (5.16), before choosing the apostles (6.12), at Peter's confession (9.18), at his transfiguration (9.29), before teaching the disciples the Lord's Prayer (11.1–3)—and, in each case, Luke inserts a phrase like 'as he was praying' into Mark or Q's source material. Of course, Jesus prays in Mark (e.g. Mk. 1.35, or 14.32–42), but Luke particularly emphasizes this habit and its power. Luke alone tells us that Jesus has prayed especially for Peter, that after his denial and turning again, he might 'strengthen' the others (22.31–32).

Watching Jesus' example makes the disciples ask, 'Lord, teach us to pray' and Luke's version of the Lord's Prayer follows (11.1–4). The parables of the friend at midnight (11.5–8) and the persistent widow (18.1–8) occur only in Luke, stressing the need not to give up, but to continue in prayer. The Pharisee and the tax-collector in the Temple, also unique to Luke, reminds us that prayer must be done in humility and forgiveness, rather than in self-righteous pride (18.9–14). In Gethsemane, Jesus asks his disciples to pray with him (22.40), as opposed to 'sit here while I pray' (Mk. 14.32; Matt. 26.36). Luke's repeated references to prayer in Acts shows that they learned the lesson (e.g. 1.14, 24; 2.42; 3.1; 4.23–31; 6.4, 6; 10.9, 30; 11.5; 12.5, 12; 13.3; 14.23; 16.13, 16, 25; 20.36; 21.5; 22.17; 28.8). Finally, Luke has contributed to the prayer of the church his songs of Mary, Zechariah, and Simeon: the Magnificat (1.46–55), Benedictus (1.68–79) and Nunc Dimittis (2.29–32).

The Holy Spirit

If the ox is the most powerful creature, the Holy Spirit is the power of God (24.49), playing a crucial role in Luke's picture of Jesus. Luke refers to the Spirit eighteen times in his gospel, with a staggering fifty-seven occurrences in Acts (compare this with the six references in Mark and twelve in Matthew!). The Holy Spirit initiates each section

of his gospel: at the beginning, the Holy Spirit comes upon
Mary (1.34), Elizabeth (1.41), Zechariah (1.67), John (1.15,
80), and Simeon (2.25, 26, 27). At the start of the ministry,
according to Luke, the Holy Spirit descends on Jesus 'in
bodily form' at his baptism (3.22), and leads him both into
(4.1) and out of the wilderness (4.14), like someone leading
an ox; 'the Spirit of the Lord is upon me' begins his manifesto at Nazareth (4.18). Similarly, as Jesus sets his face to
journey to Jerusalem, we have another cluster of references
(10.21; 11.13; 12.10, 12).

Jesus is not only supremely the man of the Spirit, but
also the one who baptizes in the Holy Spirit (3.16). In the Q
passage about asking, seeking and knocking, Matthew
concludes that God will give his children 'good gifts' (Matt.
7.11), while Luke says that the heavenly Father will give
'the Holy Spirit to those who ask him' (11.13). This
promise is renewed by the risen Jesus (24.49), and fulfilled
throughout the Acts of the Apostles (see 2.1, 33), where
Luke makes it clear that the Holy Spirit is the Spirit of
Jesus (Acts 16.6–7). Finally, although in Matthew and Mark
'signs and wonders' belong to false Messiahs (Mk. 13.22;
Matt. 24.24), in Luke, miracles reveal Jesus' identity as the
power of God: the miraculous catch of fish impresses Peter
first to confess his sin and then to follow Jesus (5.1–11).
While Jesus answers John the Baptist's question about his
identity with *words* describing his miracles in Matt. 11.4,
Luke's version has *deeds*: 'in that hour he cured many of
diseases and plagues and evil spirits' (Lk. 7.21). In Acts,
not only is Jesus 'attested to you by God with deeds of
power, wonders and signs that God did through him' (Acts
2.22), but also the apostles regularly work signs and wonders (2.43; 4.30; 5.12; 6.8; 14.3; 15.12). Luke's ox is indeed
a powerful creature of strength.

Joy and praise

'Joy', wrote C. S. Lewis, 'is the serious business of heaven.'
There is an absence of joy in Mark, arising from his theology
of suffering and darkness; his only use of *chara*, joy or

gladness, describes those in the parable of the sower who receive the word 'immediately with joy', but wither away equally 'immediately' when trouble comes (Mk. 4.16–17), while the verb *chairo*, to rejoice, is used only of the chief priests when Judas offers to betray Jesus (14.11)—not the most encouraging pair of references! While Matthew refers to joy (e.g. 2.10; 5.12; 13.44; 28.8), it is overshadowed by the pain and bitterness of the separation from Israel. Luke is well acquainted with pain, and portrays Jesus entering into the suffering of those who are burdened. However, so often those who are poor in the world's eyes have a joy which is missed by the rich and powerful. It may be just my defective knowledge of biology, but the ox does not immediately strike me as the most frolicsome of creatures—but Luke's picture of Jesus is full of joy!

Perhaps my own greatest experiences of joy have been the births of my children. Luke stresses the great joy around the births of John and Jesus: the angel promises Zechariah joy, gladness, and rejoicing at the birth of his son (1.14, fulfilled in 1.58), who leaps for joy in Elizabeth's womb (1.41, 44—*skirtao*, to leap for joy, occurs only here and at Lk. 6.23 in the New Testament). Joy issues into praise for Zechariah (1.64, 68), Simeon (2.28), and Anna (2.38). Mary's song of praise begins 'my spirit rejoices in God my Saviour' (1.47), and Jesus' birth is 'good news of a great joy' (2.10). The angels and shepherds both respond by 'praising God' (2.13, 20, *aineo*, used by Luke alone of the evangelists).

This sense of joy pervades the activity of Jesus and his followers: the seventy(-two) return from their mission practice 'with joy' (10.17), causing Jesus himself to 'rejoice in the Holy Spirit' (10.21, only in Luke). *If* Matthew's shepherd finds his lost sheep, he merely 'rejoices over it more than the ninety-nine that never went astray' (Matt. 18.13); *when* Luke's shepherd 'has found' his, he calls his neighbours for a party—'Rejoice with me'—and similar rejoicing and merry-making concludes the following parables, unique to Luke, of the lost coin (15.9) and the prodigal son (15.24–25, 32). Luke agrees with C. S. Lewis about

'joy in heaven' (15.7, 10). In another typical 'bookend', as
the gospel began in joy, so it also ends: only in Luke do the
disciples 'rejoice and praise [*aineo*] God' at Jesus' entry
into Jerusalem (19.37). When confronted with the risen
Jesus, at first the disciples 'disbelieved for joy' (24.41), but
they finish up 'continually in the Temple, blessing [*aineo*]
God' (24.53). Despite all the trials and persecutions, joy
and gladness continue on through Acts (*chara/chairo*, 8.8;
12.14; 13.52; 15.3; 16.34), as does the praise (*aineo* in 2.47;
3.8–9). So, perhaps the ox is more joyful and frolicsome
than we thought!

The sacrificial, saving victim   *The Passion, Luke 22–23*

In Luke's Passion narrative, Jesus becomes passive, like
Mark's lion being tied up and muzzled, or Matthew's
Teacher refusing to call up legions of angels. Here the reason
is divine necessity: 'it is necessary' (*dei*) appears seven
times (9.22; 13.33; 17.25; 22.37; 24.7, 26, 44; as opposed
to only once in Mark, 8.31). The bearer of burdens *must*
bear the burden to the end; the ox must go to Jerusalem to
be sacrificed.

While Matthew includes almost all of Mark's Passion,
but gives it a different atmosphere, Luke's account differs
from theirs in its details. He omits a number of incidents:
the anointing of Jesus (Mk. 14.3–9, see instead the sinful
woman with ointment in Lk. 7.36–50); Jesus' intense sorrow
in Gethsemane and the repeated sleeps (Mk. 14.33–4,
38b–42); the flight of the disciples (Mk. 14.50–2); the false
witnesses and the high priest at the trial (Mk. 14.55–61);
the silence of Jesus (Mk. 14.61; 15.4–5); the mockery by
soldiers and passers-by (Mk. 15.16–20, 29–30); Jesus' last
cry of desolation (Mk. 15.34–5); and the amazement of
Pilate (Mk. 15.44). Instead, he weaves into his account
extra material from his own sources (L), which we shall
discuss below (Lk. 22.15–16, 24–38, 43–44; 23.6–16, 27–
31, 34, 39–43, 46, 49). Also, some events are in a different
order: Jesus prophesies Judas' betrayal after the institution

of Communion (22.21–23), and Peter's denial while still at supper (22.33–4; cp. Mk. 14.29–31); the denial by Peter and the mocking of Jesus happen before the hearing (22.66–71; not afterwards as in Mk. 14.53–72). This all enables the Passion to be the climax of Luke's various storylines and themes—about the disciples, prayer, women, and the outcasts—as the burden-bearing ox becomes the sacrificial victim.

We saw earlier how Luke modelled his gospel upon a Graeco-Roman biography, particularly noting his classical preface and the birth and childhood stories. Such lives often gave the hero a 'farewell speech' before he died, taking place over a meal with his friends and including predictions about the future, his own death and the troubles ahead for his friends, exhortations to virtue, the establishment of a successor and warnings about imposters. Matthew includes some typical farewell material earlier in his great discourses (Matt. 18, 23–25). Luke begins with Jesus at table with his friends (Lk. 22.14), providing for their continuing life with the Eucharist (22.15–20), warning of betrayal (22.21–23), settling their dispute about behaviour when he is gone (22.24–30), establishing Peter as his successor to strengthen the others (22.31–34) and warning of violence (22.35–38). This farewell speech shows Jesus still caring for others and giving them help and instructions, as he has done all through the gospel. Luke has a similar farewell speech with many of the same themes for Paul in Acts 20.17–35.

In Gethsemane, Jesus the man of prayer invites all the disciples to pray with him (22.40). With his more positive description of the disciples, Luke omits Mark's mention of Peter, James and John and the rebuke to Peter; the disciples only sleep once, 'for sorrow' (22.41–46), nor do they forsake him and flee (as in Mk. 14.50). The appearances of angels at Jesus' birth (Lk. 1.26; 2.9–15) are now balanced with angelic help to face his death, stressing his human agony (22.43–44; since half the ancient manuscripts do not include them, modern commentators are divided about their authenticity). Only Luke says that Jesus healed the ear of the high priest's slave at his arrest; having helped the lowly throughout his ministry, he is not about to stop now (22.51).

For his wider Gentile audience, Luke stresses Jesus' innocence at the various hearings. There are no false witnesses, nor charges of blasphemy from the high priest (22.66–71, cp. Mk. 14.55–64). Jesus is declared innocent by Pilate three times (23.4, 13, 22), by Herod (23.15), by the penitent thief (23.40), and by the centurion (23.47)—all only in Luke. Similarly, Luke highlights the innocence of the church leaders in Acts (e.g. 4.14, 21; 5.39; 16.37–39; 18.14–15; 22.25; 23.9; 26.31). With his concern for history and geography, Luke realizes that the Roman Empire and its system of justice have enabled the church to live and grow—and his Gentile readers must understand that, although Jesus was crucified, he was no criminal.

In Luke's portrait, Jesus dies a very human death; however, he is still concerned, not for himself and his abandonment (as in Mk. 15.34), but for those for whom he has always cared, the lowly, poor, and women. After all the women in this gospel, now women are the first to weep for Jesus on his way to be crucified; as he has been concerned for them before, so now he says, 'Daughters of Jerusalem, weep not for me, but weep for yourselves and for your children'. As our television screens remind us all too frequently, it is women and children who suffer when war comes and cities are besieged—and Jesus looks ahead, beyond his own fate, to the doom of Jerusalem (23.27–31). Second, he cares for the ordinary people, the carpenters and soldiers, ignorantly carrying out the orders of the powerful: 'Father, forgive them, for they know not what they do' (23.34). Although missing in some ancient manuscripts, this fits Luke's picture of Jesus forgiving outcasts like the sinful woman (7.47–50); also, Luke shows his disciples following suit, as Stephen dies with a similar prayer for forgiveness (Acts 7.60). Third, only Luke tells us of forgiveness for the criminal crucified alongside him; once again, Jesus is concerned for the social outcasts (23.39–43). Finally, Jesus cries with a loud voice—but not in desolate abandonment: here, the man of prayer, having prayed for others (23.34), dies still trusting God, like a child saying the Jewish night psalm, 'Father, into your hands I commend my spirit' (23.46, see Ps. 31.5).

The gospel began with Mary's song of reversal for the powerful and the lowly (1.52–53), and Simeon's prophecy of division in Israel (2.34). So it ends: although the people shouted 'crucify' with the chief priests and leaders (23.13, 18), afterwards they followed Jesus to the cross with the women lamenting (23.27); they 'stood by, watching' in silence (23.35), and went home afterwards 'beating their breasts' (23.48). After all the praise in this gospel, so now a Gentile centurion praises God (23.47). The disciples did not forsake him, but watched with the women 'from a distance' (23.49). The rich and powerful have been the opponents in this gospel, and the chief priests and elders plotted Jesus' death (19.47–48; 20.19; 22.2, 52, 66; see also Cleopas' comment in 24.20); so now, it is the rulers and soldiers who mock, not the passers-by (23.35–37). The irony is in the taunt, 'he saved others; let him save himself' (23.35, 37, 39); all through the gospel, the Saviour (2.11, 30) has been concerned for others, not himself. Even now, the bearer of burdens is still trying to save the women, the ordinary squaddies, and a crucified thief—but then it always was the burden of the ox to carry the weight of others, and to be sacrificed in Jerusalem for sin.

He rides again   *The Resurrection, Luke 24*

A good ending to a story ties up the various threads; the best sort of ending opens up new horizons. Mark's gospel ended with the enigma of the empty tomb and an absent Jesus; Matthew had the supernatural happenings and the Teacher commissioning the true Israel on a mountain in Galilee, again bringing his themes together. Luke is more matter of fact: Jesus is once again walking and eating with his friends, and they stay in Jerusalem in prayer and praise in the Temple. We likened Luke's opening stories to an overture; now his coda reworks the motifs into a final, quiet movement—but, like some blockbusting movie, there is also an exciting sequel!

The women at the empty tomb do not have Mark's enigma or Matthew's fireworks (24.1–11). Without questions or earthquakes, they find the stone rolled away—and two men in 'dazzling clothes' (24.4); 'dazzling clothes' were last mentioned at the transfiguration, where two others, Moses and Elijah, talked to Jesus about his 'exodus' he would accomplish in Jerusalem (9.29–31). Now this has happened, instead of the backward journey to Galilee (cp. Mk. 16.7; Matt. 28.7), impossible for the geographically minded Luke, the women are reminded of what Jesus said 'while he was still in Galilee' (24.6)—the divine necessity of his suffering, crucifixion, and resurrection; now 'it was necessary' (*dei*) occurs three times (24.7, 26, 44) to fulfil the three passion predictions (9.22, 44; 18.31–33). Finally, Luke names those who went to the tomb, for they include Mary Magdalene and Joanna, who provided for Jesus in Galilee (24.10; see 8.1–3); with his typical understanding of women's lowly position, he points out that the men did not believe their words, 'an idle tale' (24.11)!

After the women, Luke's main resurrection story happens to two disciples, not otherwise known; again, we note his typical interest in ordinary people (24.13–35). Cleopas and his companion (wife, perhaps, to match Luke's other male-female pairings?) do not seem to believe the women's story (24.22–24). With the usual concern of the bearer of burdens, Jesus notices their sadness (24.17) and allows them to unload it on to him as he joins them on their journey— another Lukan motif. With delicious irony, they tell Jesus all about what has happened to him. Then it is his turn, and he explains the long steady view of the patient ox, 'beginning with Moses and all the prophets' (24.27). The history lesson turns into geography as they reach Emmaus, and Jesus appears to go further; as so often in this gospel with Pharisees, disciples, and sinners alike, he is invited to dinner, where 'he took the bread and blessed and broke it, and gave it to them' (24.28–30). The echo of the Last

Supper is unmistakable: immediately, the irony vanishes along with Jesus—and all that is left is a seven-mile dash back to Jerusalem to tell the others the news that Jesus can be known in the breaking of bread (24.33, 35).

The final section draws all the threads together: after vanishing at the bread course, Jesus now turns up for some fish with his friends (24.41–42), reminding us of his first miraculous catch which made them his disciples, so long ago back in Galilee (5.1–11). There is joy (24.41) and divine necessity (24.44); history and geography start to run the other way, as the remote past (Moses and the prophets, 24.44) and recent events (his suffering and resurrection, 24.46) come together for a new future, 'beginning from Jerusalem' and going away 'to all nations' (24.47). The universal Saviour, Christ the Lord (2.11) is now a revelation to the Gentiles as Simeon sang (2.32); he pours out the power of the Holy Spirit (24.49) as John the Baptist prophesied (3.16). As the gospel began, so it ends, 'in Jerusalem with great joy, continually in the Temple blessing God' (24.51–52).

And yet, like the best stories, this is not an ending but a beginning, the trailer for the sequel, for the bearer of burdens is still at work. The Holy Spirit is the Spirit of Jesus (Acts 16.6–7), and Luke's sense of the long view, history and geography is fulfilled by Jesus acting in and through the Acts of his Apostles performing the same actions in the same places and beyond, for the poor and suffering, healing and preaching the same message of universal salvation— that there is one who bears our burdens.

Figure 7 St John, *Lindisfarne Gospels*, Folio 209b.

5

The High-Flying Eagle—
John's Jesus

Farsight the Eagle   *Symbolism and meaning*

If Mark's Jesus can be seen in C. S. Lewis' Aslan the lion, perhaps there is something of John's Jesus in another Narnian character: Farsight the Eagle can fly so high and see so keenly that he can survey all Narnia as he wheels above, from the destruction of the great city of Cair Paravel in the east, to King Tirian hiding up in Lantern Waste (*The Last Battle*, Puffin/Penguin, 1956, pp. 83–85). Lewis' eagle is well-named; biologists tell us that the proportion of an eagle's brain devoted to sight is seven times greater than that in humans'. Lewis' friend, J. R. R. Tolkien, repeats the ancient myths about eagles' eyesight: 'The Lord of the eagles of the Misty Mountains had eyes that could look at the sun unblinking, and could see a rabbit moving on the ground a mile below even in the moonlight' (*The Hobbit*, Unwin, 1966, p.96). Elsewhere in Tolkien, these noble creatures are often symbols of the providence of Iluvatar, the Father of All, appearing just in time to rescue the heroes from certain death.

When I was studying in Israel, out in the Palestinian desert we used to watch these magnificent birds soaring effortlessly and steering themselves through the thermals and air currents with a disdainful flick of the tail. It is hardly surprising that ancient cultures saw them not just as the king of the birds, but as divine symbols, from the statues of the god Ninib, or Ninurta, in Assyria to the winged creatures on the pyramids. The answer of the Lord 'out of

131

the whirlwind' to Job notes its high soaring and far-seeing nature: 'Is it at your command that the eagle mounts up and makes its nest on high? . . . From there it spies the prey; its eyes see it from far away' (Job 39.27–29). God even likens himself to an eagle, telling Moses at Mount Sinai that 'I bore you on eagles' wings and brought you to myself' (Exod. 19.4). The Lord renews our youth 'like the eagle's' (Ps. 103.5) that those who wait for him shall 'mount up with wings like eagles' (Is. 40.31). The eagle is also an image of sudden speed (Prov. 23.5; Jer. 4.13; Lam. 4.19; Hab. 1.8). As a bird of prey (Job 9.26), it could be a symbol of destruction, even of God's judgement (Deut. 28.49; Jer. 48.40; 49.22). Finally, the four things the writer of Proverbs finds hard to understand include 'the way of an eagle in the sky' (Prov. 30.18–19)—which should comfort us as we seek to understand the soaring flights of St John, or find his light too bright for our eyes!

The ninth-century writer John Scotus Eriugena's 'Homily on the Prologue to the Gospel of St John' is usually known as '*The Voice of the Eagle*' from its opening words. He uses the eagle to represent the evangelist, 'the spiritual bird, fast-flying, God-seeing' ascending higher even than St Paul's vision of the third heaven as he sought to reveal the mystery of the Trinity and the Incarnation in his Prologue (*Voice*, 4–5). In our study, the symbol stands also for the portrait: John's Jesus is the eagle, while the evangelist is the visionary, caught in the eagle's talons and carried by his Lord soaring aloft. If the other gospels are like symphonies or operas, John is like a great conductor, totally absorbed in his music and straining to ensure that every theme is heard by his audience.

The high-flying perspective *Prologue and beginnings, 1.1–51*

'Let's start at the very beginning—a very good place to start.'

('Do-Re-Mi' from *The Sound of Music*)

Ancient 'lives' often began not with the subject's birth, but with his appearance on the public stage. Mark starts simply with Jesus' baptism; Matthew suggests that Jesus' public significance begins with his birth and the visit of Gentile wise men to worship him. Luke begins even earlier with the miraculous conception and birth of John the Baptist to prepare the way for Jesus. John, however, takes a quantum leap back in time. It is not enough to explain Jesus in human origins of time or place or ancestry, since he exists from *before* all time: in the beginning he was with God, and he is God (1.1). The ancient biographer Dicaearchus wrote a 'Life of Greece': John's story of Jesus is nothing less than a Life of the Cosmos! While the word *cosmos* appears a few times in the other gospels, John uses it nearly eighty times. His portrait of Jesus is painted on a cosmic scale.

In the other gospels, Jesus' story takes place in the horizontal dimensions of the geography and history of Israel; John brings in the vertical—Jesus is above and beyond all that. His place is 'with God', his time is before the beginning of everything. John takes from Greek philosophy and Eastern religion the *dualistic* distinction of the world 'above' and the world 'below', the spiritual contrasted with the physical—except that Jesus breaks it open, by coming from above into the world to save it. John paints with stark contrasts—light and darkness, truth and falsehood, life and death, love and hate, belief and unbelief, all abound through his work. Like all good conductors, he brings out the key themes strongly in this opening fanfare. The words 'life' and 'light' occur twice as often in John as in the other three gospels put together—and they are to be found 'in him' (1.4). John uses verbs of knowing, seeing and believing frequently, so they are introduced in his Prologue (1.10, 12, 14, 18); similarly, the constant theme of 'witness' or 'to testify' begins with the witness of John the Baptist (1.7–8). 'Glory' and 'truth' will reverberate throughout the story after they form the climax of the Prologue (1.14, 17).

The first section of an ancient biography usually answered two questions about the subject: who is he and where does he come from? John holds back Jesus' actual name until the very end, when he is shown to be superior even to Moses (1.17). Instead, he uses a title full of

resonances in both Jewish and Greek cultures: the Word,
Logos. The Word of the Lord was something living and
active in the Old Testament (Is. 55.11) from the creation
when God had only to speak for things to come into existence ('And God said, "Let there be . . .",' Gen.1.3, 6, 9, 11,
14, 20, 24, 26) through to the prophetic refrain 'the Word of
the Lord came to me'. In Greek philosophy, *logos* was
the logical rationality behind the cosmos; alongside this
masculine principle, the Hebrews placed the feminine figure
of Lady Sophia, the Wisdom of God, present with God at
the Creation (Prov. 8.22–31; see also the inter-testamental
Wisdom literature, such as Wisdom 7.22–10.21). John brings
all these images together in his Prologue. He deliberately
echoes the opening of Genesis with his majestic 'in the
beginning', when everything 'came into being through him'
(1.1, 3). His story of Jesus joins creation and re-creation
together: Jesus is nothing less than God, and has come from
being with God in the beginning.

And yet, the staggering thing is that this is the Prologue
to a biographical portrait of a human being. The divine
Word, in whom is light and life (1.4), was coming into the
world (1.9). After soaring to the divine heights beyond time
and space, John's Prologue suddenly swoops down to earth
to assert that 'the Word became flesh and lived among us'
(1.14). It is an extraordinary claim to make, especially
within monotheistic Judaism. 'Lived [*eskenosen*] among
us' alludes to God dwelling in the tent (*skene*) with the
Israelites in the wilderness (Exod. 25.8–9), and the prophets
longed for God again to encamp in Zion (Joel 3.17; Zech.
2.10). Furthermore, in the inter-testamental Wisdom of Ben
Sirach, the Creator tells Lady Wisdom to place her tent in
Jacob (Ecclesiasticus 24.8–10). God appeared to Moses in
the *shekinah*, the cloud of his 'glory' (Exod. 24.15ff); now
that the divine eagle has encamped in the person of Jesus,
'we have seen his *glory*, the glory as of the Father's only
Son, full of grace and truth' (1.14b). The words *charis* and
aletheia (grace and truth) reflect the Hebrew *chesed* and
'emet, God's continuing gracious love and faithfulness (e.g.
Exod. 34.6). All that the Jews had experienced and written

of the Wisdom of God the Creator is now present in Jesus, says John. 'No one has ever seen God', but he is now made known in Jesus, 'God the only Son' (1.18).

Furthermore, the Prologue also outlines the plot of the story to come. In Jesus, God has come to 'his own', his own world and his own people, and neither recognized him or accepted him. Those individuals who received and believed him became the new 'children of God' (1.10–13). Thus, despite the divine heights and the cosmic scale of this gospel, the essential storyline is the same: the mission of Jesus, how he was rejected by the Jewish leaders, and accepted by the disciples. These characters and their conflict are part of the cosmic conflict of light against darkness. Darkness, however, can neither understand it nor overcome it: the Greek *katalambanein* in 1.5 has both senses, as in the English, 'the darkness has not mastered it'. John will never leave us in any doubt as to who is in control throughout his story.

Such conflict and separation emerge immediately. Like the other gospels, John begins the main story with John the Baptist as the voice in the wilderness. However, there are crucial differences: the baptism of Jesus is never described, but merely inferred from the Baptist's comments (1.29–33). Instead of actually baptizing Jesus (which might imply that he is superior to him), John the Baptist openly witnesses to 'the Jews' and Pharisees (1.19, 24) that Jesus is superior to him (1.27, 30), the 'Lamb of God' (1.29, 36), the 'Son of God' (1.34). He even directs his own disciples to Jesus, and they follow him (1.36–37). While 'the Jews' merely ask critical questions (1.19–22, 25), several individuals do respond to Jesus' invitations, 'Come and see . . . Follow me' (1.39, 43, 46), including Simon, already renamed Peter (1.42). After swooping down from the cosmic heights, the eagle is speeding swiftly ahead, gathering some under its wings while others criticize.

'The way of an eagle in the sky'   *Following John's story,*
                                         style and structure

John and the Synoptic gospels,
sources and background

The 'way of an eagle in the sky' may be hard to understand
(Prov. 30.19) but many readers have felt similarly as they
have sought to follow the twists and turns, heights and
depths of this most subtle evangelist. As long ago as the
second century AD, Clement of Alexandria suggested that
John had composed a 'spiritual gospel' full of theological
meditation to complement the 'physical facts' contained in
the Synoptics. As we have seen, Mark, Matthew and Luke
actually have plenty of theological reflection themselves,
but John is still different. He shares the basic story of Jesus'
ministry leading to conflict with the authorities and his subsequent Passion and some sayings, stories and events are
similar to those in the Synoptics. However, he writes in a
different style, with his own themes and vocabulary, with a
different chronology (e.g. the Temple incident happens at
the beginning in Jn. 2, not at the end as in Mk. 11); there
are no parables or exorcisms; Jesus talks in extended discourses about himself rather than pithy sayings about the
kingdom of God; many well-loved characters and incidents
appear only in John—the wedding at Cana (2.1–11), Nicodemus (3.1–21), the Samaritan woman (4.1–42), the man at
the pool of Bethesda (5.1–16), the blind man at Siloam
(9.1–41), and Lazarus (11.5–44).

Interpreters of John down the centuries, assuming that he
knew the other gospels, attributed these extra elements to
his mystical imagination. Over the last half century, however, most scholars have considered John to be independent
of the others (see the source diagram in Figure 2, p. 12
above). He includes other traditions about Jesus preserved
and developed in the evangelist's church—often called 'the
Johannine Community'. Scholars have suggested various
complex theories about this group's development; many
believe that the gospel itself went through several editions
before reaching its final form. In recent years, however, the

pendulum has swung away from authorship, sources and hypothetical reconstructions of the community *behind* the text towards literary issues *in front of* the text. Such approaches accept the text as we now have it, regardless of how it came into being, and seek to explore the interaction between the text and the reader, the narrative, plot and story development, characters and conflict, style and structure— as we have been doing with all four portraits in the gospels.

Structure

The overall structure is essentially in two parts, Jesus' ministry and his Passion. The first, 'The Book of Signs', is structured around Jesus' miracles, or 'signs' as they are called here (e.g. 2.11; 4.54); it begins with the witness of John the Baptist (1.19ff.) and concludes by referring to the Baptist and to Jesus' signs in a summary (10.42). The Passion story is 'The Book of Glory', from the Last Supper (13.1) to a final conclusion (20.30–31). Although the Book of Signs seems to conclude at 10.42, another sign follows, the raising of Lazarus (11), with another summary (12.44–50)—which suggests that chapters 11 and 12 form an 'interlude' between the two halves, or possibly were inserted in a later edition. Similarly, although the gospel reaches a climax with the author's purpose in 20.30–31, the miraculous catch of fish and breakfast with the risen Christ (21.1–23) and another concluding summary (21.24–25) indicate an appendix, or later addition. The structure of the whole gospel can be pictured like an eagle, with the two main sections being the 'wings' on which it flies, separated by a thin body of material in between with the prologue and appendix forming extensions on the wingtips—feathers, perhaps? (see Figure 8).

Whether or not the prologue, interlude and appendix are later additions we cannot tell; for our purposes, they function as a beginning, middle and end around the two great major sections of Jesus' ministry and Passion.

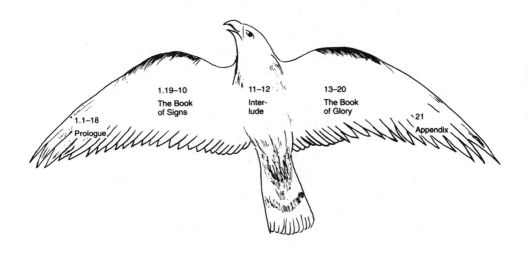

Figure 8 The structure of John's gospel

Time

For Mark the time is always 'now'; the action in his gospel occupies only a few weeks. Although Luke sets the story in a broader stream of history, Jesus still travels to Jerusalem for one Passover at which he dies, implying a ministry of only one year in all three Synoptics. The popular time-scale of three years is actually derived from John's account. Like any pious Jew, John's Jesus goes up and down to Jerusalem regularly, especially for *three* Passovers: the first is after the wedding at Cana and around the Temple incident (2.13, 23); the second takes place around the feeding of the five thousand (6.4); and the third one is constantly mentioned throughout the Passion (11.55; 12.1; 13.1; 18.28, 39; 19.14). Luke placed Jesus 'in the middle of time', between the past history of Israel and the future period of the church. John also looks back to Israel's history with references to

Moses (1.17; 5.46; 6.32; 7.19–23), Jacob (4.12), Abraham (8.32–58), and he points forward to the future church (17.20–21; 21.23–24). However, his cosmic scale runs from before time itself, 'in the beginning' (1.1) to the end of time on 'the last day' (6.35–59; 11.24; 12.48).

Time is important to the author: little words like 'now', 'already', 'just recently' abound. There is frequent mention of 'the day' and 'the hour', from Cana when 'my hour has not yet come' (2.4; see also 7.30 and 8.20) to the Passion when it finally arrives (12.23, 27; 13.1; 17.1). Literary critics distinguish between 'narrative time', the time taken to tell the story, and 'story time', the time sequence of the unfolding story. The 'narrative time' of John's story begins with a rapid blur, swifter than any eagle as we move from 'the beginning' before time to the appearance of Jesus in the eighteen verses of the Prologue (1.1–18). Then time eases up as the year between the first two Passovers passes in three and a half chapters (2.13–6.4). The next year is slower again, occupying six chapters (6.4–11.55). Finally, things slow right down with nine chapters covering one week, 'from the six days before the Passover' (12.1) until the day after it (20.1). It is as though we are watching a video, racing through the opening scenes on fast-forward, and then studying the climax in slow motion so as not to miss a single frame. The writer makes it very clear what the important things are and when they take place.

'Story time' unfolds in a steady sequence, with the occasional 'flash back' in the narrative: thus, both 7.50 and 19.39 refer back to Nicodemus' night visit in 3.2, while 18.14 refers back to Caiaphas' prophecy of 11.49–52. There are also 'flash forwards' to things which have not yet happened in the story time, although both the narrator and audience know about them: thus 'John had not yet been put into prison' (3.24); Mary is 'the one who anointed [past time] the Lord' in 11.2, even though her act is still in the story time future until 12.3. A third time frame occurs with the narrator's and audience's own day, years later. John refers forward to events which take place beyond the story time, but before the reader's time: so, the disciples remember Jesus' words about the Temple after his resurrection (2.22); the Holy Spirit 'had not yet been given' (7.39); the rumour about the beloved disciple 'spread among the community' (21.23). The flight of the eagle is very complex, soaring up and swooping down, moving forwards and backwards on the winds of the Spirit—and we must pay attention.

Style

The author has spent a long time riding these winds in his meditation and reflection, evolving a distinctive style, vocabulary, and manner of thinking. Although punctuation and quotation marks were not put into texts until the Middle Ages, 'who is saying what' in ancient manuscripts is usually obvious from the style and context—but not in John. It is even unclear who delivers his most famous verse, 'God so loved the world . . .' (3.16); some English translations give it to Jesus, continuing his speech from 3.10 down to 3.21, while others conclude his speech at 3.15, making the narrator say 3.16–21. Translations are similarly divided over whether 3.31–36 is further speech from John the Baptist, or comment from the narrator. In fact, everybody speaks the same language in this gospel, narrator and characters alike. It has a limited vocabulary, with the same key words repeating over and over again: love, truth, light, darkness, life, world, see, look, know, believe, have faith, send, abide, hour, glory, father, son. John uses these words, which are rare in the other gospels, more often than the rest of the New Testament combined. The sentences are short, building on each other in steps and stairs and spirals, often doubling back to reconnect and take the point on further. There are passages in parallel, and others in reverse (*chiasm*); sections begin and end with the same motif to form a loop or ring; numbers build up to seven signs, seven discourses, seven 'I am' sayings. Someone has thought this over time and time again, in prayer, in meditation and in teaching others.

Levels

This easy style with its repetitive vocabulary gives John's story a surface simplicity; the meditative reflection undergirds it all with hidden depths. The gospel has often been described as something in which a child can paddle, but an elephant may swim. Bright-eyed new converts are given copies to read, but its content has kept the mystics praying and the scholars arguing for millennia! This is because it functions on many levels simultaneously. When I was on study leave recently, I was privileged to watch an eagle fishing off Vancouver Island. From the beach, all I could see was the surface of the water; hovering *above* the water, the eagle could see *below* the surface—and it would dive into the water, then emerge holding the reward of fish in its talons.

As we distinguish between narrative time, story time, and the narrator's own time, so too we can see the surface level of dialogue in any incident, the deep level of its meaning within the story, and the still deeper level of the author's communication with the reader. There is a constant invitation to the reader to take the eagle's point of view, and look (and fish!) below the surface. Thus, conversations begin between Jesus and others about very human and natural things, like birth (3.3), water (4.7), bread (6.25ff.), or sight (9.1), but incomprehension and questions soon follow: Nicodemus cannot re-enter his mother's womb (3.4), the woman notices that Jesus has no bucket to get his water (4.11–12), the crowd want real bread to eat (6.32–34) and are revolted by the idea of eating Jesus' flesh (6.52). Jesus invites them to see through to the 'spiritual realities' these 'earthly things' represent (3.12), while at a deeper level still the author delivers the same invitation to the reader. Those who cannot see far or take the high perspective, like the Pharisees, remain in their blindness (9.40).

These 'misunderstandings' are crucial to John's narrative. The natural bread and water, the human birth and sight

are *symbols* of deeper spiritual realities; the surface misunderstandings are nods and winks to help the far-sighted reader
appreciate the *irony* of this gospel, while the narrative characters miss the real meaning of what is said and done. Thus,
Jesus talks about being 'lifted up' (3.14; 8.28; 12.32); the
surface meaning suggests a glorious exaltation, like a crowd
hoisting a hero on their shoulders—and this crowd asks
what he means (12.34). The reader knows that the irony
suggests the hoisting of a man on to a tortuous instrument
of death, the cross. The double irony revealed by the author
is that the hour for Jesus to be glorified (12.23) is the
Passion (13.1); what appears on the surface to be a grisly
execution is actually the glorious exaltation of the Son
returning to his Father. Caiaphas callously prefers one man
'to die for the nation' than have the Romans destroy them
all (11.50; 18.14); John points out the irony that Jesus dies
not just for the nation, but for all those who can see what
God is doing and become his children (11.51–52). Once
again, we are being invited to fly with the eagle and take
the far view and the high perspective.

All of this reveals prolonged meditation and theological
reflection by the evangelist and his community. To follow
'the way of an eagle in the sky' requires careful attention:
there will be twists and turns, wheels within wheels, sudden
changes of speed from a swift dash to a motionless hover,
movement in all dimensions and levels from the heights of
heaven to the depths below the surface. However, all this
attention and reflection is focused upon the centre-spot—
the person of Jesus. So, who is he, and what does he mean?

'The eagle has landed'?   *The person of Jesus*

The first men on the moon nicknamed their Lunar Module
'the Eagle'; as they touched down, the first words spoken
were, 'the eagle has landed'. This phrase sums up John's
Prologue: the Word of God has left the cosmic heights and
come to dwell among us—the eagle has landed. From that
moment, Jesus is nearly always centre stage. Even when he
is absent, those on stage discuss who Jesus is and what they

are going to do about him (1.19–28; 3.25–26; 7.45–52; 10.19–21; 11.45–53, 55–57; 12.9–11; 20.24–25). He dominates the text, being the subject of most of the narrative and delivering most of the discourse. He is the central character —and yet here we must be cautious. Characterization is crucial to modern literary criticism, especially the study of narrative. 'Flat' characters are dismissed as caricatures or stereotypes, while 'round' characters are carefully built up through psychological examination in modern biography, or narration of the person's internal feelings in a modern novel. However, the standard method of characterization in Graeco-Roman biographies, and in all ancient narrative for that matter, was through *indirect* means, by depiction of the subject's great deeds and words. The ancients were more interested in moral character than psychological personality, in the 'type' or example more than in the rounded individual. In the gospels, the character of Jesus is depicted not by direct analysis, but by the narration of his great deeds and words, his miracles and teaching. John has the additional difficulty of describing the human life, ministry, and death of Jesus after the sublime heights of the Prologue: so, does the eagle ever actually land?

Mark depicts Jesus as a beast of action through his miracles; Matthew portrays his Teacher through five extended sermons. John interweaves word *and* action to construct the first great 'wing' of his gospel: he calls the miracles 'signs' (*semeia*), which lead into lengthy discourses. They are not performed to show Jesus' compassion, nor is there any attempt to keep them secret: the first sign, the turning of water into wine at Cana 'revealed his glory and his disciples believed in him' (2.11); the second sign brought not just the official and his son (who was healed) to faith, but the 'whole household' (4.53). The Book of Signs concludes that John the Baptist did no signs, but now many believe in Jesus (10.41–42). The author has selected these from the 'many other signs' which Jesus did so that the reader might 'come to believe that Jesus is the Christ, the Son of God' (20.30–31).

Furthermore, while Jesus is often called teacher or rabbi

(1.38, 49; 13.13), his teaching is not about the kingdom of God, but himself. John uses all his literary skill with levels, misunderstandings and symbols to bring this out. Thus, feeding a multitude moves beyond the surface level of bread through manna and Moses down to the identity of Jesus: 'we have come to believe and know that you are the Holy One of God' (6.1–69). In typically Johannine style, the healing of the blind man progresses from the surface level of *physical* sight down to a deeper *spiritual* blindness or insight of faith, depending on differing assessments of Jesus. The Pharisees are quite sure that Jesus is 'a sinner . . . not from God' (9.16, 24)—and, ironically, this makes them blind (9.39–41). In contrast, the blind man not only receives his physical sight (9.7), but confesses his ignorance about Jesus (9.12, 25), asks for further insight and comes to faith (9.36–38). Jesus raises Lazarus so that God his Father, and himself as Son of God, might be glorified (11.4). There is John's typical use of symbolism and misunderstanding, confusing sleep and death (11.11–13). Martha misunderstands Jesus' assurance that her brother will live as referring to 'the last day' (11.24). First, she comes to believe that Jesus is 'the Christ, the Son of God' (11.27), and then Jesus asks God to answer his prayer and raise Lazarus so that the crowd might believe (11.42)—which, not surprisingly, they do when Lazarus emerges from the tomb (11.45)! The story ends with the usual irony, as the Jewish leaders plot to kill the one who gives life (11.46–53).

This combination of signs and discourses provides indirect characterization of Jesus. John builds on the symbolism with the direct statements, 'I am . . . the bread of life' (6.35, 41, 51), 'the light of the world' (8.12; 9.5), 'the resurrection and the life' (11.25); in addition 'the door of the sheepfold' (10.7, 9), 'the good shepherd' (10.11, 14), 'the way, the truth and the life' (14.6) and 'the true vine' (15.1, 5) bring us up to the inevitable seven. These 'I am' sayings are not just symbols of Jesus' identity: if we look below the surface, we see a rich Jewish background to them all. Bread and light are images of the Law and Wisdom (Ecclus. 15.3; Ps. 119.105); the vine is a symbol of Israel itself

(Is. 5.1–10; Jer. 2.21; Hos. 10.1), while sheep and shepherds describe the people and their leaders (Ps. 100.3; Ezek. 34). By applying these redolent images to Jesus, John suggests that he is the culmination of Israel's faith and history. 'I am' is God's own revelation of his name to Moses (Exod.3.14), used regularly by Isaiah (43.10, 13, 25); so, when Jesus says, 'before Abraham was, I am', they pick up missiles to stone him for blasphemy (8.58–59).

Further direct information comes through titles. Initial speculation as to whether John the Baptist is 'the Christ' is neatly redirected to Jesus (from 1.20 to 1.41, and in 3.28–30). The Samaritans discover that Jesus is the Christ (4.25–26, 29, 42), followed by further Jewish speculation (7.26–27, 31, 41–42; 10. 24). This is dangerous, for anyone who confesses Jesus as Messiah will be 'put out of the synagogue' (9.22; 12.42)—but Martha is not afraid to state her belief (11.27). John's entire purpose is that the reader might believe that 'Jesus is the Christ, the Son of God', for such faith brings life (20.30–31; 17.3). While Jesus is described as the Son of God, or the Son, eight times in Mark, ten times in Luke and fifteen times in Matthew, John uses this term twenty-five times; meanwhile God is referred to as 'Father' about a hundred times. Jesus is not only called the Son by the narrator (1.14, 18; 3.16–18, 35–36; 20.30–31), but he also uses it happily for himself, in debate with the Jews and discourse (5.19–26; 6.40; 8.36; 10.36; 11.4; 14.13; 17.1). The Jews complain to Pilate that 'he ought to die because he claimed to be the Son of God' (19.7). Indeed, Jesus even goes so far as to state, 'I and the Father are one' (10.30).

John's picture begins with the high-flying perspective of the Prologue, but throughout the narrative Jesus never loses this knowledge: he is aware of his own pre-existence with God (6.38, 62; 17.5); he knows who sent him into the world and why he was sent (6.39), when his hour has not yet come (2.4) and when it does arrive (12.23; 13.1; 17.1), what he will do when human resources run out (6.6), where he has come from and where he is going (7.33; 8.14, 21; 13.3), how he will get there (12.32–33), and the eventual destiny of all his people to be with him in his Father's glory which he had at the beginning (17.5, 24; 20.17). Such complete knowledge is indeed high-flying and all-seeing!

So, does this high-flying, far-seeing eagle actually land —is John's Jesus really human, or does he 'hover' six inches off the ground? We must recall the difference between ancient and modern characterization noted earlier. Jesus is not a rounded human character in the modern sense. However, despite his divine knowledge, John's Jesus gets weary and thirsty (4.6–7) and weeps at the death of a friend (11.35), 'snorting with rage' at what has happened (11.33, 38). Even the calm confidence of John's Passion narrative is reached through the 'troubling' of Jesus' soul in 12.27. There is the very poignant question asked by a human being who has been let down by his friends: 'do you also want to leave me?' (6.67). Such characterization by indirect hints is typical of ancient narrative, and the ambivalent tension between the divine and the human in John's Jesus is similar to the mixture of the (stereo-)type and individual character in other Graeco-Roman lives.

Unlike Mark, there is no secrecy about Jesus' identity here: it is plain from the opening Prologue (1.1) through to Thomas' confession, 'My Lord and my God' (20.28). Using Jewish legal terminology, many *witnesses* 'testify' to Jesus: John the Baptist (1.19, 34; 3.26–30); the 'one from above' (3.32–33); the Samaritan woman (4.39); Jesus' works (5.36); the Father (5.37); the scriptures (5.39); the Spirit of Truth (15.26); the disciples (15.27); the narrator himself (19.35; 21.24). However, once again John uses irony and levels of meaning: *we* know who Jesus is from the start, and we watch others coming to faith during the story. Unfortunately, many still do not perceive it because of blindness or disbelief (9.41; 10.24; 12.37). Jesus' first words are 'What are you seeking?' (1.38) and, in a flash back 'loop' or bookend, he repeats this question in the two gardens, to his arrest party (18.4, 7–8), and to Mary weeping by the empty tomb (20.15). Many people 'seek Jesus' (e.g. 6.24, 26; 11.56), but he warns both Jews and disciples that they will not find him (7.34; 8.21; 13.33). Instead,

Jesus himself does the finding—of Philip (1.43), the man at the pool (5.14), the blind man (9.35), Lazarus (11.17). Throughout the story he comes and goes as he wishes, depending on people's attitudes: Jesus seeks and finds those who come to believe in him, while those who 'seek to kill him' are frustrated (5.18; 7.19–30; 8.37–40; 10.39).

In Tolkien's *The Lord of the Rings*, 'Gwaihir the Wind-lord, swiftest of the Great Eagles' is the divine rescuer who seeks and finds Gandalf first from Saruman's imprisonment in Isengard (Unwin, 1969, p. 279), then when Gandalf fell to his death below the earth (p. 524) and finally rescues Frodo and Sam from the dark and evil slopes of Mount Doom (pp. 985–7). While Tolkien's eagles are servants of God, John's Jesus is nothing less than God himself, coming down like an eagle from the heights of the world above to save the reader from darkness and evil, if only we allow ourselves in faith to be found by him.

Talons bared for conflict   *The Book of Signs and*
                                        "the Jews", John 2–12

In Tolkien's stories, Numenor is an Atlantis-like land blessed by Iluvatar (God) which overreaches itself and turns to evil. Its doom is presaged first by eagle-shaped clouds and then by eagles themselves; few repent, so Iluvatar destroys it (*The Silmarillion*, Unwin, 1977, pp. 277–80). The eagle was also a symbol of judgement in the Old Testament. Eagles have a strong grip in their talons and they can carry away an animal from the flock; a foreign nation called by God to punish Israel 'swoops down like an eagle' (Deut. 28.49)—and the image is even applied to God himself coming in judgement (Jer. 48.40; 49.22). John's portrait of Jesus is not all soaring full of grace: both the gospel and the epistles of John bear the wounds of bitter conflict, and are not afraid to respond with beak and claw.

While the phrase, "the Jews", occurs only a few times in the Synoptics, John uses it some seventy times, particularly in the Book of Signs and the interlude as the conflict grows. The Jews first question John the Baptist (1.19, 24) and then

Jesus himself about his demonstration in the Temple at the 'Passover of the Jews' (2.13, 18–20). A 'leader of the Jews', Nicodemus, comes to Jesus by night to question him (3.1–2); later he defends Jesus, and ends up helping to bury him (7.50; 19.39). In discussion with a Samaritan woman, Jesus is clearly a Jew and 'salvation is from the Jews' (4.9, 22).

Thus, it is all the more surprising that from now on "the Jews" stand for Jesus' opponents. At a 'festival of the Jews' (5.1), they question the man Jesus healed on the sabbath (5.10, 15) and seek to oppose and kill Jesus (5.16, 18). After the miraculous feeding during another 'festival of the Jews', the second Passover (6.4), the Jews dispute with Jesus (6.41, 52), and some people stop following him (6.66). At the next 'festival of the Jews' (7.2), the conflict becomes more serious as the Jews actively seek to arrest and kill Jesus (7.1, 11, 25, 30, 32, 44–52). The people's response to Jesus is becoming divided: some speak up for him (7.12, 31, 40–41, 50–51), while others are in 'fear of the Jews' (7.13). This division continues into the next chapter where some of the Jews believe in him (8.31), yet Jesus accuses them of being 'from your father, the devil' (8.44); they respond similarly, 'you are a Samaritan and have a demon' (8.48), and attempt to stone him (8.59). The healing of the blind man accentuates the separation; while he comes to believe (9.38), his parents are afraid of the Jews (9.22), and the Pharisees, who do not believe, become blind themselves (9.18, 40–41). The Book of Signs concludes with 'division among the Jews' (10.19): some believe (10.21, 42) while others think he is demonic and try again to stone him (10.20, 31–39).

During the interlude before the Passion, the final sign brings the final division. Jesus goes to raise Lazarus, despite his disciples' warning of being stoned (11.8) and Thomas' pessimistic comment that they are going 'to die with him' (11.16). Some of the Jews mourn with Mary and Martha (11.19), see Jesus' own grief (11.36), and witness the miraculous resuscitation; as a result, 'many of the Jews' come to believe (11.45) while the chief priests and

Pharisees plan his death (11.46–53, 57). Jesus' entry into Jerusalem confirms the division: a 'great crowd of the Jews' come to see him and Lazarus, and welcome him (12.9, 12–18) and even some of the authorities believe (12.42). Meanwhile, however, the chief priests and Pharisees plot to kill Lazarus as well as Jesus (12.10–11, 19) and silence people with the threat of expulsion from the synagogue (12.42). During the Last Supper, the separation is clear: although Jesus and the disciples are all Jews, "the Jews" are now a separate group (13.33); the law is not 'ours', but 'their law' (15.25), and 'they' will expel the disciples from the synagogue and kill them (16.2). The Jews and the chief priests will bring about Jesus' suffering and death (18–19), and cause the disciples to hide behind locked doors (20.19).

The irony of this bitter portrait of "the Jews" is that the gospel itself is so Jewish. The conflicts take place at Jewish festivals, which also provide the symbols so important for John—bread at Passover (6.4–14, 25–58) and water at Tabernacles (7.2, 37–39). John begins with the incident in the Temple (2.12–25), rather than including it at the end as in the Synoptics; unlike the Synoptics, John depicts Jesus going regularly to Jerusalem for festivals, as a pious Jew. A Jewish background for author and readers alike is indicated by the only occurrences of the Hebrew-Aramaic term, *Messiah* (1.41; 4.25). When Jesus nicknames Simon 'Rocky', only John gives us the Aramaic 'Cephas' before the Greek translation 'Peter' (1.42; cp. Matt. 16.18). Jewish customs frequently appear: water jars for purification (2.6); not mixing with Samaritans (4.9); the number of witnesses needed under the law (5.31–40; 8.17); prophecy by the high priest (11.51); embalming and burial customs (19.39–40). The great heroes occur—Abraham (8.33), Isaac (3.16), Jacob (4.5, 12), Moses and the Exodus (1.17; 3.14; 5.45–46; 6.31–58; 7.38)—as well as quotations from the prophets (e.g. 12.13–15, 37–40; 19.24, 28, 36–37). Old Testament ideas and themes flow below John's surface, while its concepts of Wisdom and the Word of God, the Christ, King, and Prophet all feed into John's picture of Jesus.

How are we to explain this anti-Jewish attitude in such a gospel? Some churches now even provide apologetic explanations of Good Friday readings of John's Passion with its depiction of the Jews, lest anyone be offended. Christians should be painfully aware of anti-Jewish elements in our history and the use of the fourth gospel by Nazis to accuse Jews of being demonic (e.g. 8.44). Yet, John depicts Jesus and disciples as Jews and other Jews as believers. The development of the phrase in this gospel reflects John's typical device of misunderstanding turning to unbelief as Jesus brings division. Those who believe become followers, like the blind man (9.38) or Martha (11.27), the disciples (1.41, 49; 2.11) and the welcoming crowd in Jerusalem (12.9, 12–18). Those who do not believe become opponents, as questioning (1.19; 2.18) becomes misunderstanding (6.30, 52; 8.27), leading to blindness and plotting his death (9.40–41; 11.46–53). The divine Word enters into the world for 'his own', but 'his own' reject him (1.11); after the division among the Jews, a new group are called 'his own', loved by Jesus to the end (13.1). Essentially, therefore, the development of John's story is the same as in the other gospels: a Jewish preacher's teachings produce conflict, with the authorities as opponents putting him to death, while his followers form a new community, eventually including Gentiles, and separating from Judaism.

We saw earlier that Matthew's hostility to the Pharisees, despite his undoubtedly Jewish background, implies that the mission to the Jews was sadly past; his anger reflects the pain of the separation from the synagogue towards the end of the first century. John probably reflects a similar situation: he alone refers to the threat to be put 'out of the synagogue' (*aposynagogos*) no less than three times (9.22; 12.42; 16.2). Since Jesus and his disciples went to synagogue regularly, even in the period of Acts, these threats probably reflect the period around the *birkath ha-minim* in the mid 80s. If John's gospel is a product of complex development over many years, this explains both the Jewish background and the hostility, the familiarity and the pain. The gospel reveals knowledge of Palestinian Judaism prior to the revolt of AD 66, so the roots of John's church lie back in the Judaea of Jesus' day. After Jesus' death, further conflict ensues until the writer can use the phrase "the Jews" to symbolize all who misunderstand, disbelieve, and ultimately oppose God in Christ. The division in the story faces the reader with a decision either to join the community of faith in Jesus, or to become an opponent. It is in such conflict that the eagle's beak and talons have been sharpened—and the epistles of John suggest continuing conflict and schism (see 1 Jn. 2.18–19; 4.1–6). The gospel of John is not '*anti-*' any racial or national grouping; but, having been wounded in conflict, it pleads with the reader to make a decision '*for*' Jesus the Messiah.

Living under the shadow of his wings
Discipleship and the Last Supper, John 13–17

Like most animals, the eagle rushes into conflict when protecting its young, yet the same instinct causes it to exhibit tender care. Moses' final song compares God's concern for Israel to an eagle 'hovering over its young . . . bearing them aloft on its wings' (Deut. 32.11), echoing how God called Moses and the Israelites to Mount Sinai: 'I bore you on eagles' wings and brought you to myself' (Exod. 19.4). The 'shadow of his wings' is the Psalmist's place of refuge and hiding (Pss. 17.8; 36.7; 57.1; 63.7; 91.1, 4). While the conflict is with unnamed Jewish leaders, there is a tremendously *personal* dimension to John's portrayal of those who believe in Jesus. The disputes take place with crowds (chapters 6–8; 10), but real dialogue is with individuals, who are often otherwise unknown: Nathanael (1.45–51); Nicodemus (3.1–10); the Samaritan woman (4.7–26); the man at the pool (5.2–9, 14); the woman caught in adultery (8.9–11); the blind man (9.35–38); Martha and Mary (11.21–40); and Peter (13.6–10; 21.15–22).

John uses the term 'disciple' seventy-eight times—more often than any other gospel—but, like Luke, he has a broader interest: 'the twelve' occur rarely (6.67–71; 20.24) and 'apostle' never appears. First, various disciples are brought

by others, rather than called by Jesus himself: John the
Baptist points two of his disciples to Jesus (1.35–37); one
of them, Andrew, brings his brother, Simon Peter (1.40–42).
Philip, from the same town, is the only one to be called by
Jesus directly (1.43–44), and he then brings Nathanael to
Jesus (1.45–47). Later, Andrew brings the little boy with
the loaves and fishes (6.8), while Philip takes the Greeks to
Andrew, and then they both go to tell Jesus (12.22). The
disciples rapidly realize who Jesus is: Andrew moves from
'Rabbi' to 'Messiah' (1.38, 41), Philip sees him as the fulfilment of the law and prophets (1.45), and Nathanael goes
straight from his regional disdain—'can anything good
come out of Nazareth?'—to 'Son of God . . . King of Israel'
(1.46–49)! After Jesus revealed his glory in the first sign at
the wedding at Cana, 'his disciples believed in him' (2.11).
Like any group of disciples, they accompany Jesus (2.2;
3.22), call him 'Rabbi' (1.38; 4.31; 9.2; 11.8), and look
after his needs (4.8, 31).

The nature of discipleship is a key theme through Jesus'
debate with the Jews in the central chapters. The crisis
occurs after the feeding of the five thousand and the debate
about the bread of life: Jesus' teaching about eating his
flesh and drinking his blood is too 'hard' for 'many of his
disciples' to accept (6.60). The narrator comments sadly:
'Because of this many of his disciples turned back and no
longer went about with him' (6.66). For a moment everything hangs in the balance while Jesus asks 'the twelve'
poignantly, 'What about you? Do you also want to leave?'
(6.67). As in the Synoptic accounts of Caesarea Philippi, so
too here it is Peter who affirms their belief in Jesus as the
only one with eternal life: 'You are the Holy One of God'
(6.68). Later Jesus tells 'the Jews who had believed in him,
"If you continue in my word, you are truly my disciples"'
(8.31). None the less, the disciples are largely absent from
the central narrative while the conflict builds up (5, 7–11,
mentioned only briefly in 9.2 and 11.7–16). The conflict
with the Jews is one Jesus himself must endure; he has
come to 'his own' (1.11), and it is only when they reject

him that the disciples come centre-stage as 'his own' to be loved to the end (13.1).

Given John's use of misunderstandings and levels of meaning, it is not surprising that, like everyone else, the disciples misunderstand Jesus from time to time. Only after the resurrection do they understand his saying about the Temple, and 'they believed' (2.19–22). When they bring him food, he explains that doing God's will is meat and drink to him (4.31–33). Those disciples who stay at the surface levels of eating his flesh and drinking his blood find his teaching too hard and leave him (6.60, 66). Jesus explains to his disciples that suffering is not caused by sin, but is to reveal God's activity (9.2); similarly, Jesus moves them on from Lazarus' physical sleep and death to life and God's glory (11.4, 11–15). They do not understand the deeper meaning of his entry into Jerusalem on a donkey until after his resurrection (12.16). However, John never develops this misunderstanding into Mark's criticism of the disciples—quite the reverse. While others may turn back, they realize there is nowhere else to go and remain loyal (6.67–69). They 'continue in my word' (8.31): even if it means certain death, doubting Thomas still urges them to go with him (11.16). When Jesus is hiding from the Jews, they are with him (11.54). By the end of the Book of Signs, the division is complete: the Jews' misunderstanding leads to blindness, opposition, and the plot to kill Jesus, while the disciples believe, despite their misunderstanding, and are ready to follow him into hiding and even death.

This mixture of faithful following with levels of (mis-) understanding is best exemplified through the Last Supper and the Farewell Discourses (13–17). John indicates its importance by slowing narrative time right down: after the several years of the Book of Signs, now seven chapters describe just twenty-four hours; John is really making a meal of it—literally! The institution of the Eucharist is omitted; instead Jesus washes his disciples' feet in a final, desperate attempt to explain his deeper meaning, to prepare them not just for his betrayal, death and departure, but also for the whole history of the church. He keeps telling them things *now* for their *future* guidance (13.19; 14.29; 15.11; 16.1, 4, 33). For the last time, the eagle gathers its young under the shelter of its wings, cleans them and encourages them; tomorrow it will be pierced through the breast—and they will have to fly by themselves.

Chapter 13 provides the context for the content of the Farewell Discourses (14–17) with the usual symbols, misunderstanding and different levels. The narrator begins by pointing out the deep meaning to the reader: Jesus loves 'his own' ultimately, 'to the end' (13.1). The foot-washing is a symbol of Jesus' ministry (13.8–10), but also an example of loving service for his disciples to follow (13.14–17), which is not understood 'now . . ., but later' (13.7). They do not understand his warning of betrayal (13.22), nor going away (13.33); first Peter (13.36), then Thomas (14.5), Philip (14.8), and the other Judas (14.22) ask where he is going and what he means. The promise that they will see him again brings more confusion (16.17–19). When finally they claim to understand, Jesus warns them that they are about to be scattered in a last attempt to give them peace and courage (16.29–33) before turning to pray for them (17).

The content of the farewell is an extended meditation on the unity and love between Jesus and his Father in the Spirit, applied to his disciples. Like all farewells, there is a last wish, that after his demonstration of the foot-washing they should 'love one another, as I have loved you' (13.34–35; 15.12–17). Jesus and his Father dwell in each other through love (14.10–11, 20; 16.28), and through the Spirit they will dwell in the believer who abides in them (14.15–17, 23, 26; 15.1–11); the Spirit will guide them in truth (15.26; 16.7–15). Although he warns of troubles and sufferings ahead (14.1, 27, 30; 15.18–25; 16.1–4, 20–22, 32), Jesus encourages them with his peace and the promise of future security under his wings (14.1–3, 18, 27; 15.18; 16.20–24, 33). Finally, he concludes with an extended three-fold prayer: for God to be glorified in himself (17.1–5); for the disciples to be protected (17.6–19); and for all those who believe to come at the end to the glory which he had at the beginning with the Father (17.20–26).

Two other figures at the Last Supper attract our attention. *Peter* was brought to Jesus by his brother, rather than being called directly and Jesus renames him immediately, rather than after his confession (cp. 1.42 with Matt. 16.18). As in the Synoptics, Peter blurts out his faith in Jesus (6.68–9) and the same impetuous character misunderstands the foot-washing, first refusing Jesus, then eagerly wanting a full bath (13.6–9)! Similarly, he rashly swears to follow Jesus to the death (13.36–38), lashes out with his dagger in the garden (18.10), and ends up denying that he is a disciple before cock-crow (18.17, 25, 27); although not the first at Jesus' tomb, he is the first to rush in (20.6). Only John tells the story of his three-fold reinstatement, recalled back from his old way of life, fishing, to care for Jesus' sheep and lambs, leading eventually to the martyr's death Peter had rashly promised at the Last Supper (21.1–19).

While this coheres with the Peter depicted in the other gospels, here he is overshadowed by the unnamed '*disciple Jesus loved*'. He only appears in the Book of Glory, as a 'bosom friend' intimately next to Jesus at the Supper, whom Peter requests to find out about the betrayer (13.23–26). At the foot of the cross, he is the only disciple to witness the crucifixion, and Jesus entrusts his mother to his care (19.25–27; 35). He outruns Peter to reach the tomb first, and is the first to believe (20.2–8). When fishing with Peter, he recognizes the risen Jesus on the shore; Jesus tells Peter that this disciple's fate is none of his business (21.20–23). Also, we have an unnamed 'other disciple' who gets Peter into the house of the high priest, whom he knows; only Peter denies Jesus there (18.15–17). The identity of this mysterious 'Beloved Disciple' is greatly debated. The final verses of the gospel appear to be confirmation by church leaders that he has been the authority, if not the author, behind the story (21.24–25). This clue has traditionally identified him with John, son of Zebedee, never named in this gospel and just referred to in 21.2. If the gospel went through several versions over a long period of time, the apostle John may have been the original story-teller, whose preaching brought this church into being—but from the text, we simply cannot know.

Whatever his identity, the 'one whom Jesus loved' plays the part of the ideal disciple while the Farewell Discourses reflect ideal discipleship (14–17). John's community would resist any suggestion that Peter is superior to their Beloved Disciple, while the narrator invites us to respond to Jesus as he does. The Jews fail to understand Jesus, and oppose him. The disciples sometimes misunderstand him, but follow him. Peter makes rash promises of faith, but serves him. This unnamed disciple is faithfully present at all the climactic events, and is loved by Jesus. The narrator opens his symbolism to the listener, while the author reveals his levels of meaning to the reader, so that we might put our name to this character and become 'the disciple Jesus loves'. The eagle beckons, for yet there is room under the shelter of its wings to rest our head upon its breast.

The hour of glory   *The Passion, John 18–19*

The sight of an eagle climbing up into the sky is glorious. So, too, for John, the death of Jesus sets him free of the earth to return to his Father on high; the hour of his Passion is also the hour of glory. This is the supreme irony. As always, John's narrative functions on several levels with continuing misunderstanding. On the surface level, the Jews, as Jesus' enemies, bring about his arrest, trial and ignominious death; for the reader, who sees below the surface, it is the *world* which is on trial. Jesus is mocked as king, yet his kingly glory is revealed at the deeper level—he is all they say, and more.

Mark's Jesus becomes increasingly passive, as the lion is muzzled into silence to be mocked and killed. This passivity is explained by Matthew (fulfilment of scripture, and Jesus' own choice) and Luke (divine necessity). However, eagles are pretty hard to restrain, and John's Jesus is actively in control throughout the Passion. The narrative begins with his total knowledge from this high perspective (13.1–3) and *he* sets the pace. The nearest we get to the agony in Gethsemane is his soul being 'troubled' (12.27). Jesus is in control, and he chooses to lay down his life of his own volition (10.18). Knowing what is going to happen (13.1–3), he explains it all to his disciples in the Farewell Discourses of 14–17. He carries his own cross 'by himself' with no mention of Simon of Cyrene (19.17) and his suffering is not stressed. Instead, he continues to direct affairs from the Cross (19.26–30). Jesus has been in control thoughout this gospel, and he remains in control even at his death.

The story begins in a garden, as it will also end in a garden (18.1; 19.41). Gethsemane is not named, nor is it a place of agonized prayer; Jesus simply goes there to be arrested. Judas arrives with the soldiers, 'with lanterns and torches' to remind us of the night (13.30; 18.3). Judas does not identify Jesus; instead, Jesus is in control, knows everything and takes the initiative with his question, 'whom are you seeking?' (18.4). When they reply, 'Jesus of Nazareth', he answers, 'I am' (18.5). Again John mixes levels of narrative: while *ego eimi* can mean 'I am (that person)', 'that's me', it is also the phrase of divine revelation, linked to all the other 'I am's in this gospel. No wonder, then, that the soldiers, instead of grabbing the person they wish to arrest, fall to the ground in awe at the divine Name (18.6). Jesus takes control and encourages them to arrest him and let the disciples go (18.7–9). Only John tells us that Peter makes the rash attempt with a sword, and names Malchus (18.10). Despite Jesus being so much more in control—or perhaps because of it—only John mentions the binding of Jesus (18.12). The attempt is made to clip the eagle's wings—but we know that it is futile.

At the trial, several themes re-emerge. Jesus described himself as the good shepherd laying down his life for the sheep, unlike the thief and robber, and the door for the sheep to the yard or fold (*aule*), protected by the gatekeeper (10.1–11). Now Judas, 'the thief' (12.6), has come to the garden (18.2), and Jesus' sheep have gone. Jesus is taken to another yard (*aule*), guarded by a gatekeeper (18.15–16).

While Jesus is on trial for his identity—'I am'—in the same yard, Peter fails *his* trial by denying his discipleship—'I am not' (18.17, 25, 27). The Jews, his opponents all along, are responsible for Jesus' death, preferring Barabbas, 'a robber' (18.40). While Pilate tries to save Jesus several times, the Jews are insistent on his blood (18.31, 38b; 19.4, 6, 12, 15). After so many references to truth in this gospel, Pilate still does not know it when he faces the incarnate Truth (18.38; cp. 14.6). They discuss true kingship (18.33–39; 19.3, 15) as Jesus informs Pilate that real power comes 'from above' (18.36; 19.11). The irony is that Jesus, mocked with a crown of thorns and a purple robe (19.2), really *is* 'King of the Jews', as Pilate's superscription for the cross declares in all languages (19.19–22). As he prophesied, he is now 'lifted up' (3.14; 12.32); as statues of 'Christus Rex' depict him with crown and robes while nailed to the cross, Jesus reigns from the tree.

Now he fulfils scripture: his clothes are left intact (19.24) to fulfil Psalm 22.18; however, Mark's cry of abandonment from the same Psalm does not fit this atmosphere. When I was in the Palestinian desert, we had to drink three litres of water a day—and similar amounts are recommended even for package holiday makers to Greek islands. Jesus hangs in this Mediterranean heat, but says 'I am thirsty' to fulfil scripture (19.28, see Ps. 69.21). Similarly, the piercing of his side instead of his bones being broken fulfils the law about the paschal lamb and other prophecy (19.36–37; see Exod. 12.46; Num. 9.12; Zech. 12.10). After all the 'witnesses' in this gospel, the Beloved Disciple receives the care of Mary and witnesses blood and water flowing from the spear-wound (19.26–27, 34–35). Thus, there is no need for the Synoptics' centurion; the ideal disciple has been the faithful witness to the end, and now he explains the significance of it all.

Nor is there any darkness in John. The gospel which has used the dualism of light and darkness ever since the Prologue does not need a physical eclipse of the sun. When Judas left the Supper, 'it was night' (13.30); but 'those who walk at night stumble' (11.10), and so they bring torches to arrest him (18.3). However, those who walk in the light see through to the heart of the final irony: although Jesus' final cry of *'tetelestai'* might suggest that all is 'finished' at the surface level, in reality now everything is 'accomplished' (19.30). *The Lord of the Rings* comes to 'the end of all things' in terrible darkness for Sam and Frodo on Mount Doom when the 'journey is finished' and the evil of the Ring is finally destroyed; our heroes collapse, facing certain death from the smoke and fire, lava and ash. Yet this is also the moment of salvation, when 'Gwaihir saw them with his keen far-seeing eyes' and the three great eagles swoop down to rescue them and bear them away to the land of healing (Unwin, 1969, pp. 983–7). So also John's eagle cannot be bound, but flies in glory towards the light with healing; he has been in control throughout—and now everything he came for is finally 'accomplished'.

'Risen with healing in his wings'
The Resurrection, John 20–21

Tolkien's eagles provide one last example. At the battle with the evil Balrog on the bridge of Khazad-dûm, Gandalf the wizard sacrifices himself for his friends and falls to his death with the foe, 'darkness took me, and I strayed out of thought and time'; eventually, 'Gwaihir the Windlord found me again', and the great eagle restores him to his friends, alive and even more powerful as Gandalf the White (*The Lord of the Rings*, Unwin, 1969, pp. 348–9, 524). So, too, John's Jesus, who is so much in control, sacrifices himself in the struggle with evil on the cross—only to rise again. His account of Jesus' death depicted everything gradually stripped away until we reach the numbing grief of the burial in a new tomb in a near-by garden (19.41–42). The resurrection story must now offset this emptiness, and bring about the climax and closure of the whole story.

John's resurrection stories have neither Mark's enigma nor Matthew's supernaturalism; Jesus is as much in control as he has always been. He appears when *he* wishes, to Mary in the garden (20.14), to the disciples in the locked upper room (20.19), to Thomas in his doubts (20.26) and to the disciples back in their old way of life, fishing (21.4). Even though the fishermen in their grief can see nothing on the surface, from his high-flying perspective Jesus can see below to where the fish are, just like the eagle I saw fishing off Vancouver (21.6). However, he can also see far into the distance to what kind of death Peter will die (21.18–19), and what will happen to his Beloved Disciple (21.22–23). This control, knowledge, and direction of events is not new, not a product of the resurrection; it has been the character of John's Jesus from the very start, 'in the beginning' in the Prologue. Now the epilogue repeats and concludes all this master story teller's themes.

The Psalmist rejoices 'in the shadow of his wings', but the prophet foretells that 'the sun of righteousness shall rise, with healing in its wings' (Mal. 3.20/4.2). As throughout his ministry in the Book of Signs, so now in risen glory, Jesus brings healing to those in need: as Mary weeps, he whispers her name and brings comfort (20.11–17); to the disciples locked into fear and locked in by fear, he comes with peace and joy (20.19–21); for Thomas trapped in doubt, he offers his hands and side in tangible proof (20.24–29). Supremely, in a narrative echo of the opening stories, now he comes to Peter painfully mindful of his triple denial, bringing three-fold restitution (21.1–17). From the first chapter to the last, the call is the same, 'follow me' (1.43; 21.19, 22). Throughout the gospel, Jesus calls God 'the one who sent me'; now he commissions them, 'as the Father has sent me, so I send you' (20.21). Like the Samaritan woman and the blind man, even now those who receive his touch become his witnesses to others: unlike Mark's silent, frightened women, Mary obediently announces the resurrection to the disciples immediately (20.17–18).

Images of sight and blindness, light and darkness, seeking and finding have recurred throughout this gospel. When Gandalf the White reappears to his friends, they do not recognize him: 'might we know your name?' (*The Lord of the Rings*, Unwin, 1969, p. 515). Similarly, Mary can barely see through her tears and supposes at the superficial level that the mysterious figure is the gardener. Jesus repeats his first words in this gospel, 'whom are you seeking?' (20.15, cp. 1.38). As so often, he invites a deeper look to discover his real identity, 'Come and see' (1.39, 46). When Mary obeys Jesus and goes to the disciples, she announces, 'I have seen the Lord' (20.18). When they 'see' the Lord in the locked room, the disciples rejoice (20.20). Thomas refuses to believe unless he 'sees' the wounds; after he finally sees and believes, Jesus blesses 'those who have not seen and yet have come to believe' (20.24–29). Similarly, the disciples do not recognize the stranger on the shore; only when they see the miraculous catch of fish in their net does the deeper realization come, 'It is the Lord!' (21.7). In each case, seeing leads to a recognition of Jesus' identity as Lord, with Thomas making the fullest confession, 'My Lord and my God!' (20.28).

For the reader who has taken the higher perspective, this truth has been known from the start. The Word who was God in the beginning is now acknowledged as God at the end. Resting effortlessly on its wings, the eagle has wheeled around full circle. Its journey has taken it from the heights of the Prologue to the depths of the earth, and back again. All that has happened is that the divine has returned to the divine, and the eagle to its nest in the bosom of the Father. And if tracing 'the way of the eagle in the sky' sometimes causes us to labour all night and yet catch nothing, it is to such disciples that the risen Jesus comes to heal, forgive, and restore—and to invite us to breakfast on the fish held in his grasp.

Figure 9 Four Gospels, One Jesus
Westminster Abbey Psalter, *c.*1200

6

. . . One Jesus?

This book began with four pictures of Churchill—the
statesman in conference with his allies, the family man at
tea, the man of war with the chaps, and the quiet painter on
holiday. Despite certain common elements, like the cigar,
each picture was very different, and communicated a different story—yet all were of one and the same person. We also
suggested that the gospels are forms of ancient biography
with Jesus as their subject; as such, their Christologies—
their differing pictures of Jesus—must be the key to their
interpretation. Therefore, the four main chapters traced
these four portraits of Jesus, as different as our four pictures
of Churchill: the lion of St Mark, bounding on stage,
rushing around and roaring enigmatically, and dying terribly
alone; the human face of St Matthew's Teacher of Israel
with his long sermons, being rejected, and forming a new
community of faith; the patient beast of burden of St Luke,
caring for all, especially the outcasts, right up to and including his sacrificial death; and the high-flying, far-seeing,
all-knowing eagle of St John. Now, finally, we must consider
the issue which inevitably follows: what is the relationship
between the plurality and the unity, between the four gospels
and the one Jesus?

Four portraits or four Jesuses?

The first question concerns whether there are four gospels
and one Jesus, or four Jesuses. Is there any unity between
the portraits? How can we respect their diversity, yet seek
the one person behind them? The four living creatures of

163

Ezekiel and Revelation were applied to the evangelists by the Fathers and in the Celtic illuminated gospels. The *Book of Kells* uses them particularly to adorn its Canon-tables—columns of chapters and verses acting as a guide to parallel or similar passages in other gospels. Despite such cross-references, these tables still preserve the four gospels separately, and the artists depicted the four symbols separately at the top of the tables. There is no tendency to coalesce the four figures into one fabulous creature—the so-called 'tetramorph' (meaning 'four-form'), which occurs sometimes in mediaeval art. Crashing the four into one mish-mash is reminiscent of Tatian's *Diatessaron* of the late second century, a single narrative account weaving sections from all four gospels together with no regard for their differences.

The temptation to construct one 'master-narrative', or to use one gospel only, was very strong for the early church. The plurality of four gospels, four lives of Jesus, and hence four Christologies, was clearly a problem. Non-Christian critics like Celsus, Porphyry, and Julian were quick to point out the differences; the mere existence of several accounts suggested that not one was perfect. This probably explains why Irenaeus made his convoluted attempt in *Against the Heresies* III.11.8–9 to justify four gospels by reference to the four corners of the earth, the four winds, the four living creatures, and the four covenants. Continuing efforts were made from Origen to Augustine to defend this plurality. Significantly, the early church set its face against both Tatian's harmonizing approach and Marcion's exclusive use of one gospel (Luke), preferring instead to preserve four gospels separately within the canon of the New Testament.

Clearly, it does not respect the evangelists' carefully crafted portraits, nor their preservation by the Fathers, if today we simply crash them into one harmony, or not so harmonious lowest common denominator. In Chapter 1, we suggested that this is as absurd as a portrait of Churchill entertaining Roosevelt to tea wearing a painter's smock over half a uniform. Instead, each picture must be appreciated on its own, and individual attention given to its image or message. Thus, we have tried to delineate each portrait separately, using the four symbols to guide our reading. They provide a convenient aid for the memory, to help us hold the overall picture of each gospel in mind when reading any particular part. Individual gospel passages should be read always in the context of this primary biographical aim—namely, to tell the story of this particular person in this particular way: 'what is this passage trying to say about the person of Jesus?; how does it contribute to the overall picture?; and how does the overall picture help us understand this passage?'

Second, we need to be cautious about mixing the individual passages too easily, as often happens at carol services or Good Friday meditations. We have seen that Matthew has particular literary and theological purposes in his story of the wise men, such as kingship, worship, and powerful Gentiles coming to Jesus; similarly, Luke's humble scene with the shepherds at the back of the inn sets his theme of Jesus bearing the burdens of the lowly. If we bring the two groups together into a stable (not mentioned in any gospel!), the themes will clash and neither will be properly appreciated. Similarly, Mark depicts the desolation of Jesus on the cross with his single cry, 'My God, my God, why have you forsaken me?' (Mk. 15.34); John, however, stresses his cry of triumph, 'It is accomplished' (Jn. 19.30). Both represent the culmination of their respective gospel's portraits and theologies. We cannot enter into the horror of the first, nor feel the power of the second, if they are narrated together in liturgy.

Third, in many churches, we do not concentrate enough on each gospel in turn to appreciate its nuances and theology. The joint lectionary of Sunday readings, used in the Church of England and other Protestant churches, jumps around from gospel to gospel every week; however, reading chunks of about ten to twenty verses at a time from different gospels will not build up the whole picture in people's minds. It is not surprising that this system is now under review by the Joint Liturgical Group. Interestingly, both the Roman Catholic lectionary and the Episcopal Church in the USA use a three-year cycle, with all the readings taken from *one* Synoptic gospel each year—and using John for Easter and feasts. This does allow each portrait, with its own special concerns, to be built up in the listeners' minds over the course of a year. It also encourages preachers to work through a gospel commentary and to link their sermons together, teaching their people.

Thus, both the evangelists themselves and the early church wanted to preserve four different gospels, each with their own literary and theological purposes in their different portraits of Jesus. It is all the more striking, then, that although the evangelists clearly feel free to alter things to build up their own portrait of the hero, nonetheless, all four still tell essentially the same story: the ministry of Jesus from his baptism to his death, narrating his great deeds and words, healings and teachings in Galilee and in Jerusalem. Responses to him differ, with some believing and following Jesus, while others oppose him—which leads to similar plot-lines in each gospel. The conflict is between Jesus and the religious leaders of his day, which will eventually result in the formation of the church out of the disciples. Jesus is described in exalted language as Christ, Lord, or Son of God. Eventually, he comes to Jerusalem and is arrested by Jewish leaders, but executed on a cross by Roman authorities— and something odd happened afterwards. There are four gospels, with four pictures, telling four versions of the one story of Jesus.

From four gospels back to one Jesus

This basic unity of story outline within the plurality of portraits brings us to the second set of questions regarding the relationship of the four images to the search for the historical Jesus: what continuity is there between Jesus himself and the portraits? Do we talk of *Mark's Jesus*, implying that this is his own creation—or of *Mark's view of Jesus*, implying roots in a historical person whom the evangelist has appreciated in a particular way. Do the evangelists *select* appropriate material from their sources, or *create* it themselves? What is the relation between 'his story' and 'history' —and can 'his story' be true if it is not 'history'?

John has Pilate ask, 'What is truth?' (Jn. 18.38). Even today, with all our technology of cameras and recorders and verbatim transcripts, there is still debate among academics about the meaning of historical truth, and differences in the media between docu-drama and documentary, fiction and faction. We must not transfer these modern concepts to ancient texts without considering their understandings of truth and myth, lies and fiction. To modern minds, 'myth' means something untrue, a 'fairy-story'; in the ancient world, myth was the medium whereby profound truth, more truly true than mere facts could ever be, was communicated. The opposite of truth is not fiction, but lies and deception; yet even history can be used to deceive, while stories can bring truth. This issue of truth and fiction in the ancient world is too complex to cover in detail here. However, the most important point to remember is that the ancients were more interested in the moral worth and philosophical value of statements than their logical status, in truth more than facts. Pilate's question reflects the fact that the words 'true' and 'truth' occur about 45 times in John's gospel.

Unfortunately, the debate between so-called 'conservatives' and 'liberals' about authenticity is often conducted in twentieth-century terms. As one student asked me, 'Why does John keep fabricating material about Jesus despite his expressed concern for the "truth"?' However, the negative connotation of 'fabrication' is modern. Let us illustrate this point by looking at another ancient biography, the *Life of Agricola*, Roman governor of Britain from AD 78 to 84, written by his son-in-law, the famous historian Tacitus. One quarter of the entire book is devoted to the final battle between the Romans and the Britons on a hillside somewhere in Scotland; Tacitus is not concerned to give us the basic facts, like the date or place of this crucial showdown. Instead, we have two long speeches delivered by the opposing generals to encourage their troops for battle. While his father-in-law might have reminisced to Tacitus about his speech, the speech by Calgacus, the Caledonian chief, is clearly the 'fabrication' of Tacitus (*Agricola* 30–32). It is extremely unlikely that an ancient Briton would have known about half of the Roman behaviour mentioned, let alone be able to denounce it in beautifully balanced Latin rhetoric—but neither Tacitus nor his audience would have dreamt of applying the modern connotations of 'fabrication' to his work. The force of terse, pithy comments like '*solitudinem faciunt, pacem appellant*' ('they [the Romans] create a wilderness and call it peace', 30.5) is true, and an ethical challenge to Tacitus' audience, even if Calgacus could never have said it. This is the important 'truth' for Tacitus, not mere 'facts', like the time or place of the battle.

If the gospels are biographical portraits of Jesus, we need to study other ancient biographies and their relation to their subjects. Just as the number of gospels brings plurality to the accounts of Jesus, so too we have groups of Lives about other ancient subjects, such as Socrates the philosopher, or Cato the Roman politician. Ancient writers distinguished clearly between history writing (which included a significant degree of interpretation anyway) and *encomium*, or 'eulogy', written to praise someone, often in defiance of the facts. From the perspective of literary genre, biographers operated between these extremes. They were allowed more interpretation of their subjects than in history writing, but they did not go to the lengths of encomium or the early novel; there had to be a correlation of the account with the historical person. This indicates the room for manoeuvre the evangelists have in creating their pictures of Jesus: we should not expect modern criteria of history, but nor the creativity of legend or novel.

Unfortunately, some modern studies assume that if there is 'fiction' in the gospels, then they are inauthentic or unreliable. However, closer attention to literary criticism shows that no-one wrote a classical biography to provide a documented historical text—but rather in an attempt to get 'inside' the person. Even today, many biographies have an imaginative element. Thus, John's stress on 'truth' is not about 'documented fact', but the 'higher truth' of who Jesus is—which is why he writes in a biographical format. For him, Jesus is 'the way, the truth and the life', so his Jesus says these words (Jn. 14.6), just as Tacitus' Calgacus condemns Roman imperialism, or Matthew's Jesus speaks from a mountain as another Moses. To ask whether either Jesus or Calgacus actually ever spoke those words is to miss the point completely. These are not lies or fiction—they are ways of bringing out the truth about the subject which the author wishes to tell the audience.

This interpretative function of biography is dismissed by some modern critics, who prefer to 'peel away' the evangelists' layers in an attempt to reconstruct the 'historical Jesus'. However, to strip away Calgacus' speech as Tacitus' invention is to lose both its literary significance in the narrative and its historical significance in Tacitus' work. Such an approach risks committing the reductionist fallacy. To call Exeter Cathedral 'nothing but a pile of stones', peeling away centuries of meaning and interpretation, or to describe a human being as 'nothing but a pound's worth of chemicals and a bucket of water' or 'a collection of selfish genes', is to miss their significance. The statements are true at the lowest level of meaning, but other levels of meaning cannot be so reduced. To treat the four gospels like the proverbial onion from which we peel away layers to reveal the one Jesus as 'nothing but a Jewish prophet', not only risks having nothing left at the centre, but also misses the significance of their biographical genre. These interpretative layers reveal the impact which this *person* has had upon the writers.

Of course, historical reconstruction is important. The nineteenth-century 'Quest for the Historical Jesus', and the 1950s/60s 'New Quest' produced various pictures of Jesus, some more convincing than others. More recently, new attempts have been made to set Jesus in his contemporary social and historical context. Some have likened him to a wandering philosopher or Cynic in a Hellenistic background. A greater consensus among scholars currently sets Jesus firmly in his Jewish setting as an eschatological prophet. Like many others, Jesus preached and taught a radical stress on the activity of God, coming to challenge and to judge his people. This is what Jesus called the kingdom of God—or, as it is better translated, the kingship of God; the parables are all about what happens when God is recognized as King, rather than a particular territory or place. He preached the need for repentance to prepare for the kingdom/kingship, but stressed God's gracious love and free acceptance of sinners and even outcasts. This attitude, exemplified in his demonstration in the Temple, brought him into conflict with the religious authorities, who took him to the Romans for crucifixion, assuming that would be the end of the story, as it had been with so many other disruptive prophets. Unfortunately, it was not; fired by their belief that God had raised Jesus from the dead, his followers expanded rapidly—and so we move into the history of the early Christian communities and their eventual separation from Judaism.

Some reconstructions of Jesus end up with an innocuous figure who fits so well into the Jewish background that it is hard to see why anyone should have crucified him. Others stress the significant role which Jesus saw for himself in actually bringing in the kingdom of God through his ministry and, supremely, through his death. This vision of God so gripped all his teaching and preaching that this intensely theological Jesus will always require interpretation, so his meaning and purpose are more significant for the 'truth' than mere facts. Instead of peeling away the evangelists' layers, we need them to reveal the impact Jesus had upon people and why his followers believed he was still alive. We require an historical 'core' to start it all off and to explain what produced these four extraordinary portraits.

In Mark, Jesus' identity is revealed through supernatural means, the demons and the heavenly voice, and confirmed finally by the centurion at the cross: 'truly this was the Son of God' (Mk. 15.39). In Matthew this leads to the worship of Jesus, from the wise men at the birth (Matt. 2.2,11), through the disciples in the storm-tossed boat (14.33) to the new community on the mountain (28.17). Luke makes the remarkable shift from using *ho kurios* to mean 'the Lord God' in the early chapters to making it his main term for Jesus; what God is, Jesus is. John makes this explicit, from the Prologue—'the Word was God' (Jn. 1.1)—right through to Thomas' confession—'My Lord and my God' (20.28).

All four agree that in his deeds and words Jesus acts and speaks for God. He is not just a prophet, nor even the human agent of the kingdom of God; for the extraordinary response is that of worship, worship which may only be given properly to God himself. There may be four gospels, but there is only one Jesus, and he is God.

From four gospels forward to many Jesuses

Many interpretations tend to create the subject's portrait in the author's own image. Irenaeus applies the four living creatures not only to the evangelists themselves, but also to their portraits of Jesus: the four symbols are 'images of the disposition of the Son of God', depicting something of the meaning of Jesus—the lion his royal power, the ox his sacrifice, the human his human coming, and the eagle his Spirit (*Against the Heresies*, III.11.8–9). Just as you cannot have history without interpretation, so you cannot have biography without characterization. When the subject has changed the author's life, and the author writes to change the reader's, interpenetration of author, subject, and reader are inevitable. When the author believes that the subject is still alive and inspiring his writing, creative development will ensue. In fact, there is something elusive about Jesus of Nazareth; as the authorities discovered, just when you think you have nailed him down or even piled large stones on top of him, he has a tendency to pop up again in unexpected places!

So, we should not be surprised if various reconstructions of the historical Jesus are in vogue for a while and then get redefined. This has been the story of Christology all the way through. While Tatian's *Diatessaron* enjoyed some popularity as a single 'master-narrative', the second and third centuries saw the production of many accounts of Jesus. Some of these may have shared the biographical genre, although their remains are too fragmentary to be certain (e.g. *The Gospel of the Nazarenes* or *Ebionites*). Others, such as the *Gospel of Thomas* were just collections of sayings with no narrative framework at all. Still others

tried to fill in the missing years with legends about the
infancy or childhood of Jesus (with stories such as Jesus
making clay birds fly), or going even further back to tell
the story of Mary (*Protevangelium of James*). These two
tendencies—either to reduce the gospels down to one master-
narrative or to multiply accounts infinitely—produced great
arguments through the late second, third, and fourth centuries as the early church grappled with the New Testament
canon and the definition of Christology, the nature and
person of Jesus. On the one hand, keeping four gospels in
the New Testament meant that plurality was permissible
within the canon. On the other, the Christological debates
of the early councils tried to set some limits to the understanding of Jesus.

Eventually, the Council of Chalcedon in AD 451 produced
the orthodox Christological formulation that Jesus was one
person with two natures, human and divine—attempting to
hold together both elements we noted in our four portraits.
However, such a statement reflects the move of the church
out into the Graeco-Roman world; from the wandering
Jewish rabbi and prophetic agent of God's kingdom, Jesus
is now being described in the language of Greek philosophy.
Such Christological development is inevitable as the portraits of Jesus are reinterpreted and incarnated in successive
cultures. The ensuing centuries produced yet more plurality
with innumerable images of Jesus. Early mosaics depict
Jesus as a youthful, clean-shaven, curly-haired shepherd,
caring for his people. Understanding shifts as the powerless
man on a cross becomes first the ruler of the Roman Empire
under Constantine, and then the Byzantine 'Pantocrator',
the controller of the universe. Artistic representations keep
pace as Jesus is clad in the purple of the imperial toga,
followed by the long-haired, bearded figure in white robes
who stares sternly at us from mediaeval frescoes and icons.

With the Renaissance of the fifteenth and sixteenth centuries, Jesus became the 'Universal Man', depicted with a
new realism by the likes of Michelangelo, Raphael and El
Greco. As the Reformers translated the gospels into the
vernacular languages of Europe, so Luther insisted that

religious art must reflect the humanity of Jesus as the mirror of the eternal God: Johann Sebastian Bach picked up this stress with his heart-rending settings of the *St Matthew Passion* and *St John Passion*, while Albrecht Dürer used his own face to paint Jesus (*Self-portrait, c*.1500). There can be no clearer demonstration of the interpretation of the subject in the image of the author. The Age of Reason brought the post-Enlightenment rational Jesus in the seventeenth and eighteenth centuries; David Hume dismissed the miracles, and scholars like Reimarus and Lessing began the quest for the historical Jesus, a human teacher once more, to be compared with the likes of Socrates. In the following century, *Lives of Jesus* are written with Romantic idealism, while Holman Hunt paints a bearded, crowned figure disconsolately knocking on the overgrown door of the soul, yet staring pleadingly at the beholder in his *The Light of the World* (Keble College, Oxford, 1853). As the missionary movement spread across the world, Jesus became the man of all cultures, sitting cross-legged in Indian robes or taking tea with his disciples in a Chinese willow pattern.

Finally, in our own century, the nineteenth-century Liberal gives way to Jesus the Liberator. Paul's claim that in Christ there is 'neither Jew nor Greek, neither slave nor free, neither male nor female' (Gal. 3.28) has motivated movements from the abolition of slavery to the ordination of women. From Dietrich Bonhoeffer in prison for his part in conspiring to murder Hitler to Catholic priests fighting oppressive regimes in South America, the question is asked whether the Liberator comes with a gun as an optional extra; yet the great modern apostles of non-violence, like Gandhi and Martin Luther King, also claimed Jesus as inspiration. Graham Sutherland's *The Crucifixion* in St Matthew's, Northampton, painted just after the Second World War, identifies Jesus with the suffering of the world, while his great tapestry of *Christ in Majesty* in Coventry Cathedral, brimming with 1960s confidence, takes us back full circle to the Jesus seated on high ruling the universe. But we have also had the Nazi Jesus, shown as blue-eyed and pure Aryan; while, from pop culture, in Andrew Lloyd

Webber and Tim Rice's *Jesus Christ Superstar* Mary
Magdalene sings, 'he's a man, he's just a man', yet cannot
understand why he affects her so. Subsequently, Jesus even
became the prophet of wealth creation in Mrs Thatcher's
famous exegesis to the Church of Scotland's General
Assembly of the good Samaritan being able to buy private
health care for the wounded man!

From the four gospels, we have moved forward to many
different Jesuses in theology and in culture, in faith and in
art. Inevitably, the final issue returns to interpretation: are
all these portraits equally valid? Can Jesus be reincarnated
in every generation like this? Are we free to create, and
recreate, Jesus in our own image, to pick and choose Christology à la carte for the consumer society? Or, are there
limits?

Plurality within limits

If we return to our initial comparison with Churchill, then
certainly Lady Churchill believed that there were limits
with regard to portraits of her husband, although the criteria
seem subjective. Graham Sutherland's tapestry of Christ
can still be seen at Coventry, but his infamous portrait of
Churchill she destroyed because she did not like it. On the
other hand, plenty of caricatures and cartoons of Churchill
survive at Chartwell. Some are recognizably part of the usual
mix, while others stand outside that tradition, such as Nazi
propaganda, which may still have the common identifying
feature (such as the inevitable cigar) and yet depict an image
which has no continuity with either historical evidence
nor the development of the other pictures. Thus, we can
use these two criteria—the historical evidence and the
development of the tradition—in assessing the plurality of
interpretations of Churchill.

Equally, we have four gospels in the New Testament, not
one—which implies plurality and diversity in our views of
Jesus. On the other hand, there are only four, not forty-
four—which implies limits to the plurality; other portraits,
such as the apocryphal and gnostic gospels', were not

accepted into the canon of the New Testament. The early church wanted to keep four distinct separate portraits of Jesus, while at the same time setting boundaries for future pictures. Robert Morgan has suggested that such plurality should be seen not as a problem, but as a theological opportunity, both for historical and doctrinal reconstruction, and as an incentive to produce more 'faith images of Jesus', with the canonical gospels acting 'both as a stimulus and a control' for that process (*Interpretation* 33.4, October 1979, p. 386). Therefore, we must resist the typical response to plurality going back to Tatian's *Diatessaron*, namely harmonization into a single master-narrative or mish-mash; the four gospels act as a 'stimulus' to new pictures. At the same time, they also act as a 'control' upon this process: Irenaeus suggested that there had to be *four*, no more and no less. Even if we are not persuaded by Irenaeus' argument about the four winds or four corners of the earth, a canonical approach still leaves us with the interesting number of four.

Some have suggested that the four gospels represent four *sources*, the teaching of the four apostolic missions: that of James in Matthew, Peter in Mark, Paul in Luke, and John in John. Others have gone to the other end of the process with four intended *audiences*, Matthew to the Jews, Mark to the Romans, Luke to the Greeks, and John for the church. My symbolic reading of the four portraits suggests that the plurality may allow for different *temperaments*: Matthew's human Teacher will attract those interested in law and teaching, and in getting things clarified and tied down; Mark's enigmatic lion may help those in the darker experiences of suffering; Luke's hard-working ox will appeal to people labouring for liberation among the oppressed; while the flights of John's eagle will enchant the mystics. The four gospels have even been linked to the four *personality functions* of Jungian psychology, used in Myers-Briggs analysis: thus, Matthew is the 'thinking gospel' full of logic and order; Mark is the 'sensing' gospel with its vivid and graphic immediate narrative; Luke is the 'feeling' gospel with its concern for the burdened; and John is the 'intuitive' gospel with its flights of metaphor and symbol.

Thus, the plurality of four gospels provides a stimulus for the many images of Jesus produced over millennia; they can also help stimulate new images of Jesus for our post-modern, even post-atheistic, world facing the twenty-first century after the collapse of optimistic scientific humanism in the West and communism in the East. But what about the limits? How do the four gospels provide any 'control' over these pictures? Interestingly enough, four is also the number of sides for a playing field or ball park. Whether the game is soccer or American football, rugby or baseball, the ball must stay within the field to be in play; beyond the limits is out of bounds and a 'line-out' or 'throw-in' is needed to put the ball back in play. To hit the boundary may score a 'six' in cricket or 'home run' in baseball—and everybody stands up and applauds; but the ball must still be retrieved and returned to the field of play for the game to continue.

This is exactly how the classical statements of Christian doctrine function, by providing 'fences' or boundaries. The doctrine of the Trinity does not define the nature of God (for who can describe him?), so much as set limits for orthodoxy. If you go too far past the 'three-ness' limit, you become 'tri-theist', with three separate gods at odds with the biblical monotheistic tradition. On the other hand, if you overstress the 'one-ness', you end up 'modalist', with one God operating in three modes, which causes problems such as the Father suffering and dying on the cross, with no one left to oversee the universe on Holy Saturday or bring about the resurrection on Easter Sunday! Similarly, the classic 'two nature' doctrine of the incarnation does not tell us everything positively about Jesus, but provides negative tests: if you say he is just a man or a human prophet on the one hand, or conversely that he is God who never really touches earth, then you have parted company with the Christian tradition.

So, can the four gospels, with their different Christologies symbolized by these living creatures, define the ball park, and help us place both the one Jesus and the many portraits? By opting for *four* pictures, rather than one, in the Christian tradition, the early Fathers provided a spur to the production of new images of this person in every generation. By selecting *only* four, they mapped out the ball park where those who wish to remain in the tradition must play. If we concentrate on hitting one boundary, perhaps by a brilliant exposition of just one gospel, people may stand and applaud—but the game cannot continue until we return to the middle. Somewhere *in between* the four boundaries, running around on the field of play but refusing to be tied down, is the historical Jesus whose character stimulated it all in the first place. Many of the other pictures of Jesus down through history have also played their part and contributed to the game within these four accounts.

However, some images have gone outside these limits; thus, Jesus the cultural imperialist often exported along with Western colonial expansion, is in direct contradiction to the four gospel texts, with their stress on Jesus being among the poor and lowly. Similarly, Jesus the armed revolutionary or the Aryan racist have parted company with the biblical tradition of Jesus bringer of peace for all nations, and are thus not valid interpretations. Some contemporary reconstructions of Jesus as the Divine Spirit do not take seriously his *humanity* portrayed in all four gospels. Equally, attempts to see him as just a human prophet, whether as in the Koran or some Jewish traditions, or in some modern scholarly reconstructions, do not do justice to the *worship* given him in the texts. The early church may have constructed the Chalcedonian definition of one Jesus in two natures in terms of Greek philosophy, but this was an attempt to stay within the ball park, loyal to the portraits in the gospels. Docetic Christologies, where Jesus was a divine person who only *appeared* to be human (from the Greek, *dokein*, 'to appear') were outside the limits on one side; adoptionist Christologies, with Jesus as a human prophet adopted by God at his baptism, went beyond the texts in the opposite direction. Both interpretations lie behind many modern understandings of Jesus; however valid these may be in their own terms, they are beyond the field of play mapped out by the four gospels, and outside the Christian tradition. Thus, 'four gospels, one Jesus' can provide both plurality *and* limits, stimulus *and* control.

Biography, faith and worship

This book has attempted a symbolic reading of the narratives of the gospels as biographies of Jesus. Biography is a form of story, and human beings find their identity through stories, which brings a community dimension to interpretation. There is an inevitable triangle of relationships in any communication: the author, the text, and the reader—or the storyteller, the story, and the audience. Families define themselves by the old stories of individual members told at family gatherings; social groups recount their history through members' stories. The two great stories of the church tell of the Creation and the Incarnation. Biography is an ideal literary genre, for it creates meaning and incarnates it in a human life. The Judaeo-Christian tradition has always had a strongly materialistic dimension, rooted in its doctrine of Creation. This positive attitude allowed early Christian writers and communities to create a subgenre of classical biography to express their understanding of Jesus of Nazareth. Other religious groups or philosophical schools defined their self-identity by telling stories of their founder. For the first Christians, however, the resurrection made the enormous difference: for the hero of the story was not a dead founder, but a living presence among them now, inspiring, creating and re-creating the story by his Holy Spirit. God had become real, had been earthed in the person of Jesus—incarnated, to use the later technical term. Now Jesus had to be earthed in the story, and the story fleshed out in narrative—theology incarnated in biography.

Study of the gospels, whether within scholarship or the churches, should never forget this dimension. Often, it is concerned only with issues *behind* the text, such as the sources or communities which preserved the traditions about Jesus, or the content and themes *within* the text, like the kingdom of God. In our triangle of relationships, we must also be aware of those who stand *in front of* the text, the reader or listener. Whatever its sources, content or audience, biography is written essentially by people, about people, for people. All good portraits confront us with a person, and elicit a response from the beholder. As the four pictures of Churchill lead back to the man himself, and stir feelings within us, so too the four gospels press the question: what sort of person is this? where did he get this authority?—and, most telling, what are *you* going to do about him? This study has suggested that, despite their plurality of portraits, the four gospels confront us with one Jesus—with the understanding that what Jesus is, God is. In each case, the response sought from the reader is the same—faith, which leads to worship: 'my Lord and my God!' (Jn. 20.28).

The lion, the human, the ox and the eagle are the four faces of the cherubim who support the throne of God in Ezekiel's visions (Ezek. 1.10; 10.14). Similarly, the four living creatures are around the throne of God in the Revelation of St John (Rev. 4.7); whenever these four give glory to God, the response of the angels, elders, and myriads around is to fall down and worship (Rev. 4.10; 5.8, 11,14). At the End, these four symbols make sense only within the context of worship. Like the intricate pictures of the *Book of Kells*, St Mark's bounding lion, St Matthew's human Teacher of Israel, St Luke's burden-bearing ox, and St John's high-flying eagle help us illuminate the four gospels and appreciate the one Jesus.

Suggestions for Further Reading

CHAPTER 1: FOUR GOSPELS

On gospel criticism

Richard A. Burridge, *What are the Gospels? A Comparison with Graeco-Roman Biography*, SNTS Monograph Series 70 (Cambridge University Press, 1992). The revised version of my doctoral thesis demonstrating that the gospels are a form of ancient biography.

Christopher Tuckett, *Reading the New Testament: Methods of Interpretation* (London: SPCK, 1987). A helpful introduction to all the various critical tools applied to the whole New Testament.

On the various versions of the symbols in the Fathers

T. C. Skeat, 'Irenaeus and the Four-Gospel Canon', *Novum Testamentum* 34.2 (1992), pp. 194–199. A clear and concise discussion of Irenaeus.

For theological heavyweights, the classic discussion (in German of course!) remains Theodor Zahn's appendix 'Die Thiersymbole der Evangelisten', pp. 257–275 of volume II *Der Evangeliencommentar des Theophilus von Antiochen* in his series *Forschungen zur Geschichte des neutestamentliche Kanons und altkirche Literatur* (Erlangen: Andreas Deichert, 1883).

On the illustrated gospel manuscripts

George Henderson, *From Durrow to Kells: The Insular Gospelbooks 650–800* (London: Thames and Hudson, 1987). The most comprehensive discussion with lots of black and white photographs.

For the individual books, see for example, Janet Backhouse, *The Lindisfarne Gospels* (Oxford: Phaidon, 1981) or Peter Brown, *The Book of Kells* (London: Thames and Hudson, 1980), both of which include plenty of illustrations.

CHAPTERS 2–5: THE GOSPELS

The following are some useful and accessible books, available in paperback, which cover more than one gospel.

Graham N. Stanton, *The Gospels and Jesus* (Oxford University Press, 1989). Probably the best introduction available; Part I looks at each gospel in turn, Part II considers the issues about Jesus.

Stephen C. Barton, *The Spirituality of the Gospels* (London: SPCK, 1992). A most helpful treatment, reaping the positive benefits of scholarship to reveal each evangelist's understanding of the presence of God in Jesus.

Jack Dean Kingsbury, *Jesus Christ in Matthew, Mark and Luke* (Philadelphia: Fortress Press, 1981). Looks at Jesus, discipleship and soteriology in Q and the three Synoptics.

J. L. Houlden, *Backward into Light: The passion and resurrection of Jesus according to Matthew and Mark* (London: SCM, 1987). A fascinating translation of critical scholarship into a set of Holy Week addresses, full of insights.

F. J. Matera, *Passion Narratives and Gospel Theologies: Interpreting the Synoptics Through Their Passion Stories* (New York: Paulist Press, 1986). Takes Mark, Matthew and Luke in turn, giving an overview and commentary on each Passion narrative related to its gospel's theology.

CHAPTER 2: MARK

Commentaries

Morna D. Hooker, *The Gospel according to St Mark*, in the Black's New Testament Commentaries Series, (London: A & C Black, 1991). A readable and accessible commentary, with good up to date discussion on most areas.

Robert A. Guelich, *Mark 1–8.26*, Word Biblical Commentary, Vol. 34A (Dallas: Word, 1989). A good, recent commentary on the first half of the gospel.

Eduard Schweizer, *The Good News According to Mark* (London: SPCK, 1971). This remains a classic.

On Mark's narrative technique

Robert C. Tannehill, 'The Gospel of Mark as Narrative Christology' in *Perspectives on Mark's Gospel*, *Semeia* 16 (1979), pp 55–95. The classic essay which started this approach to Mark as a story about Jesus.

David Rhoads and Donald Michie, *Mark as Story: An Introduction to the Narrative of a Gospel* (Philadelphia: Fortress, 1982). A fascinating study of Mark's rhetoric, settings, plot, and characters from a literary perspective.

For further reading on Mark and his themes

Christopher Tuckett (ed.), *The Messianic Secret*, Issues in Religion and Theology 1, (London: SPCK, 1983).

William Telford (ed.), *The Interpretation of Mark*, Issues in Religion and Theology 7, (London: SPCK, 1985). Both of these books collect together various significant articles from the 1960s and 1970s, prefaced with a helpful introduction to their topics.

Jack Dean Kingsbury, *The Christology of Mark's Gospel* (Philadelphia: Fortress, 1983). Considers the various theories about Jesus' identity, including Son of God and Son of Man.

Ernest Best, *Mark: The Gospel as Story* (Edinburgh: T & T Clark, 1983). Contains brief and clear introductions to all the main areas of Mark—anything by Best on Mark is always worth reading.

References to the Narnia Chronicles in Chapter 2 are to the stories by C. S. Lewis, in the Puffin editions published by Penguin Books, Harmondsworth, sequentially 1959–1965, and reprinted frequently since.

CHAPTER 3: MATTHEW

Commentaries

Eduard Schweizer, *The Good News According to Matthew* (London: SPCK, 1976). A refreshing combination of theological and spiritual insight.

W.D. Davies and Dale C. Allison, *The Gospel According to St Matthew* in the International Critical Commentary Series (Edinburgh: T & T Clark; Vol. 1 1988; Vol. 2 1991; Vol. 3 forthcoming). This is going to be the definitive commentary for the future; it is demanding, based on the Greek text, and expensive—but well worth consulting in a library. Vol. 1 contains an extensive Introduction to all the main areas.

On Matthew's content, themes and narrative

Graham N. Stanton (ed.), *The Interpretation of Matthew*, Issues in Religion and Theology 3, (London: SPCK, 1983). Another useful collection of major articles, with an excellent, clear introduction to Matthean scholarship from the editor.

Graham N. Stanton, *A Gospel for a New People: Studies in Matthew* (Edinburgh: T & T Clark, 1992). Provides an up to date introduction, plus chapters discussing various approaches to Matthew, different themes of the gospel, and the background to the separation of church and synagogue.

R. T. France, *Matthew – Evangelist and Teacher* (Exeter: Paternoster Press, 1989). A detailed discussion of all the main areas, with a careful consideration of traditional views and modern scholarship.

Jack Dean Kingsbury, *Matthew as Story* (Philadelphia: Fortress Press, 1988 revised second edition). Applies narrative study to Matthew's treatment of Jesus, the disciples, and the Jewish leaders.

CHAPTER 4: LUKE

Commentaries

C. F. Evans, *Saint Luke* (London: SCM, 1990). Contains over 100 pages of introduction to the main areas, plus 800 pages of commentary, which makes it quite expensive for a paperback, but it contains the author's life's work and is full of helpful insight.

Joseph A. Fitzmyer, *The Gospel According to Luke*, Anchor Bible Vol. 28 on Lk. 1–9 and Vol. 28A on Lk. 10–24 (New York: Doubleday, 1981/1985). This has one of the best Introductions around, followed by detailed commentary and notes.

On Luke's theology and interests

Hans Conzelmann, *The Theology of St Luke* (Harper & Row, 1960; Philadelphia: Fortress Press paperback edition, 1982). The English version of the better-titled *Die Mitte Der Zeit* (1953/57), the classic study of the role of history and geography in Luke's theology of salvation.

Robert F. O'Toole, S.J., *The Unity of Luke's Theology: An Analysis of Luke-Acts*, Good News Series 9 (Delaware: Glazier, 1984). A good clear introduction to every area of Luke's theology.

Robert C. Tannehill, *The Narrative Unity of Luke-Acts: A Literary Interpretation*, Vol. 1 (Philadelphia: Fortress, 1986). Applies narrative criticism to Luke's account of Jesus, the people, disciples and authorities; Vol. 2 goes on to Acts.

CHAPTER 5: JOHN

Commentaries

Raymond E. Brown, S.S., *The Gospel According to John*, Anchor Bible Vol. 29 on Jn. 1–12 and 29A on Jn. 13–21 (New York: Doubleday, 1966/1970). The classic, with a full introduction to the issues and masterful commentary on the text.

George R. Beasley-Murray, *John*, Word Biblical Commentary 36 (Dallas: Word, 1987). A good recent commentary in a traditional format, available in paperback.

Mark W. G. Stibbe, *John*, Readings Series (Sheffield Academic Press, 1993). A new reading of the whole text from a narrative-critical viewpoint, looking at the plot, structure, characterization, and context of each section.

On the background, theology and narrative of John

John Ashton (ed.), *The Interpretation of John*, Issues in Religion and Theology 9 (London: SPCK 1986). The usual selection of historically significant articles prefaced with an introduction.

Barnabas Lindars, *John*, JSNT New Testament Guides (Sheffield Academic Press, 1990). A brief and accessible introduction to the main issues regarding the study of the fourth gospel.

Stephen Smalley, *John – Evangelist and Interpreter* (Exeter: Paternoster, 1978). Provides fuller coverage of all the major areas.

R. Alan Culpepper, *Anatomy of the Fourth Gospel: A Study in Literary Design* (Philadelphia: Fortress, 1983). This brought about the revolution away from background issues to study of narrative, plot, characterization, implicit commentary, and the role of the reader.

References to J. R. R. Tolkien's stories in Chapter 5 are to the following editions:

The Hobbit, London: Unwin paperback third edition 1966.
The Lord of the Rings, London: Unwin one volume India paper edition 1969.
The Silmarillion, London: Unwin hardback first edition 1977.

CHAPTER 6: ONE JESUS?

On the development of the Canon of the New Testament

Harry Y. Gamble, *The New Testament Canon: Its Making and Meaning* (Philadelphia: Fortress Press, 1985). A brief and clear account, with pp. 24–35 dealing with the gospels.

Bruce M. Metzger, *The Canon of the New Testament: Its Origin, Development, and Significance* (Oxford: Clarendon, 1987). A full and detailed discussion of all the evidence in the Fathers; see especially pp. 262–4 on 'The Plurality of the Gospels' and pp. 296–297 on the differing orders of the gospels.

On research into the historical Jesus

E. P. Sanders, *The Historical Figure of Jesus* (Harmondsworth; Allen Lane, Penguin, 1993). The most accessible recent account; see also his *Jesus and Judaism* (London: SCM, 1985) for further detail and scholarship.

N. T. Wright, *Who was Jesus?* (London: SPCK, 1992). A lively short paperback, with a brief summary of the various Quests, a critique of certain popular views and an outline of Wright's reconstruction; for the full scholarly treatment see Wright's *The New Testament and the People of God* (London: SPCK, 1992) and *Jesus and the Victory of God* (London: SPCK, 1996).

On ancient ideas of truth

Christopher Gill and T.P. Wiseman, (eds.), *Lies and Fiction in the Ancient World*, (Exeter University Press, 1993). A stimulating collection of papers covering many different types of ancient literature – except, unfortunately, biography!

C. B. R. Pelling, 'Truth and Fiction in Plutarch's *Lives*', in D. A. Russell (ed.), *Antonine Literature* (Oxford University Press, 1990), pp. 19–52. A good, clear discussion of the issue in one ancient biographer.

On the many portraits of Jesus

J. L. Houlden, *Jesus: A Question of Identity* (London: SPCK, 1992). An accessible discussion of Christology, from the New Testament via the early church and Chalcedon to today's debates.

Jaroslav Pelikan, *Jesus through the Centuries: His Place in the History of Culture* (Yale University Press, 1985). A most readable and fascinating account of the various accounts of Jesus from the earliest days until the twentieth century.

Denis Thomas, *The Face of Christ* (London: Hamlyn, 1979). A coffee-table book with lots of pictures of the different frescoes, paintings and sculptures of Jesus.

On the plurality of the gospels

Oscar Cullmann, 'The Plurality of the Gospels as a Theological Problem in Antiquity' in his collection *The Early Church: Studies in Early Christian History and Theology*, ed. A.J.B. Higgins (Philadelphia: Westminster Press, 1956), pp. 37–54; translated from the original German article in *Theologische Zeitschrift*, i (1945), pp. 23–42.

The journal *Interpretation*, volume 33.4 (October 1979) contains helpful articles by Charles H. Talbert, 'The Gospel and the Gospels', pp. 351–362; Jack Dean Kinsgbury, 'The Gospel in Four Editions', pp. 363–375; Robert Morgan, 'The Hermeneutical Significance of Four Gospels', pp. 376–388.

Index